OXFORD
INDIA SHORT
INTRODUCTIONS

BOLLYWOOD

The Oxford India Short
Introductions are concise,
stimulating, and accessible guides
to different aspects of India.
Combining authoritative analysis,
new ideas, and diverse perspectives,
they discuss subjects which are
topical yet enduring, as also
emerging areas of study and debate.

For more information visit our website:
https://india.oup.com/content/series/o/
oxford-india-short-introductions/

OXFORD
INDIA SHORT
INTRODUCTIONS

BOLLYWOOD

M.K. RAGHAVENDRA

OXFORD
UNIVERSITY PRESS

OXFORD
UNIVERSITY PRESS

Oxford University Press is a department of the University of Oxford.
It furthers the University's objective of excellence in research, scholarship,
and education by publishing worldwide. Oxford is a registered trademark of
Oxford University Press in the UK and in certain other countries.

Published in India by
Oxford University Press
YMCA Library Building, 1 Jai Singh Road, New Delhi 110 001, India

ISBN-13: 978-0-19-946933-8
ISBN-10: 0-19-946933-4

Typeset in 11/15.6 Bembo Std
by Excellent Laser Typesetters, Pitampura, Delhi 110034
Printed in India by Replika Press Pvt. Ltd

For Pia and Bharat

'The cinema substitutes for our gaze a world more in harmony with our desires.'

—André Bazin

Contents

Introduction
The Hindi Film and Its Significance

Film and Reality

It is a truism to say that cinema began as an extension of photography, an imprint of actual reality taken by a mechanical device. It began with the very humble invention by Louis Lumière, who devised a way of synchronizing the shutter movement of the camera with the movement of a strip of photographic film. The Lumières were manufacturers producing photographic film, and this is all that Louis Lumière did as an inventor; but he also envisaged cinema as a way of recording real life in movement. The first showing of films by the Lumières to a paying public was on 28 December 1895 in Paris and lasted half an hour.

By this time, Louis and his brother Auguste had made about 50 short films, the very first one showing workers leaving the Lumière factory in Lyon, shot from the window of the house on the opposite side. All these films were recordings of public events, such as a head of the state arriving for a reception, or scenes from family life, like their father playing cards with his friends. Among those invited to that screening in 1895 was George Méliès, a magician and illusionist, who saw other possibilities in Lumières's 'cinematograph'. The story goes that when Méliès was filming with his primitive camera, the film jammed and it took a few moments for the camera to resume working. By this time what was in front of the camera had changed, but the camera continued to record what it was seeing. Thus, in the developed film, Méliès saw that a bus turned into a hearse and men into women.

Where the Lumières saw the cinematograph as a way of recording reality, Méliès saw it as a way of promoting illusion. The stream of images that a cinematograph created were taken for 'reality' even when they were the result of tricks, and that made it ideal for magic. Among Méliès's films were *The Man with the India-Rubber Head* (1902), in which a mad scientist removes his head and blows it up like a balloon until it explodes, and *The Melomaniac* (1903), in which a man juggles with his own head. Méliès also adapted fairy tales and stuffed them with inventions like these.

Out of these two polarities in cinema—its capacity to capture real life and its propensity to sustain illusion—emerged the two ends without which cinema is (almost) unimaginable. Since cinema began as a capture of reality, it was ideally suited to follow mimesis, which had been the basis of much of Western art and literature. Mimesis, in the Aristotelian sense, means the imitation of what one perceives through the senses in the physical world, but it also implies a degree of subjectivity. In cinema, this means that apart from capturing reality, there needs to be expressivity, or making something of reality so that it is comprehensible to others. It is not enough to capture reality as a continuous flow of images, as it cannot exist independently of the observer. There needs to be distortion of some kind—either through cutting and splicing bits of film or set design/mise en scène to make the film correspond to the artist's view of the real world. This is where the illusion-producing tricks of Méliès were useful. If early cinema enabled the capture of reality or the creation of illusion, later cinema hovers between 'realism' and 'expressionism' (or 'formalism'), between capturing reality and shaping it cinematically, in order to accommodate a subjective view of captured reality.

Dada Saheb Phalke and the Case of Indian Cinema

Dhundiraj Govind Phalke, or Dada Saheb Phalke as he is usually called, is credited with making the first Indian feature film *Raja Harishchandra* (1913). The film may have run to about an hour, although (according to the *Encyclopaedia of Indian Cinema*) only 1,475 ft of the original film still survives. The other silent fiction films by Phalke to have survived in bits and pieces (running to less than three hours in all) are *Pithache Panje* (1914), *Lanka Dahan* (1917), *Sri Krishna Janma* (1917), *Kaliya Mardhan* (1919), *Sant Eknath* (1926), and *Bhakta Prahlad* (1926). Phalke envisaged the future of Indian cinema very differently from the ways suggested by the Lumières and Méliès. He reportedly saw a film called *The Life of Christ* around Christmas in 1910 and became excited at the prospect of seeing 'Indian images' on the screen. There are various interpretations of Phalke's choice of the mythological film as the genre to begin Indian cinema with, but an aspect generally agreed upon is that the primary aesthetic influence was the painter Raja Ravi Varma (1848–1906). A parallel between Phalke's work in films and Ravi Varma's work in oil painting has been suggested, since both of them attempted a recreation of a mythical past to reclaim it as a nationalist proposition; this is despite Ravi Varma using a naturalistic format derived from European oil paintings and Phalke's films using a 'frontal' aesthetic derived from the Parsi theatre of his times.

There are seeming contradictions in Phalke's choices to make mythological films as staged plays without embracing Ravi Varma's naturalistic approach (in his scenes from mythology), while also insisting that he was being 'realistic'. If Phalke, who was preoccupied with establishing and nurturing an Indian film industry, was also intent upon bringing 'Indian' images to the screen—these were not just any Indian images—his aim was to introduce the traditional sacred into the space of the colonial 'modern'. He did not use Western modes of film, which were visually closer to Ravi Varma's images, because it was not enough for cinema to give physical shape to mythology; the sanctity of myth had also to be emphasized.

Unlike in a painting, there is the possibility of an actual encounter in theatre, and this encounter between audience and actors was what Phalke attempted to harness. Although Phalke was familiar with cinema from the West, he used a camera style that corresponded to a recording of staged performance or to Parsi theatre, in which there is no imaginary fourth wall and the actors face and make eye contact with the audience. (This is in contrast to naturalistic theatre, in which actors conduct themselves as though there is no audience.) This 'style' used by Phalke has been attacked by critics like Chidananda Dasgupta for not being cinematic, but there is adequate evidence that it was deliberate. There are other films of his contemporaries, films in which mythological stories are told more naturalistically, like Baburao Painter's *Muraliwala* (1927), in which there is a sense of the camera being placed within the space occupied by the characters. But in this tale, set in Krishna's childhood, the 'godly' aspect of the child is overlooked, something that Phalke would not do as, for instance, in *Kaliya Mardhan*, one of his own versions of Krishna's story.

In speculating about why Phalke used the frontal camera instead of using a more naturalistic style closer to Ravi Varma's pictures, we need to take his claim that his films were 'realistic' seriously. Obviously they were not realistic in the way that the Lumière films were, and they do not even promote illusion the way Méliès's films do, because they are shot on tacky sets with men playing female roles, and this is not true of Baburao Painter's films which are closer to the Lumière kind of realism. An explanation offered by theorists is that the frontal style depended on the concept of 'darshana' in which the deity or the priest has to give his/her blessings to the devotee who faces him/her. When Phalke tried to provide the public with 'real' manifestations of their beliefs and to 'bring the known alive', he chose this frontal mode of film-making as that was closest to the sacred, temple encounter. To Phalke, being 'realistic' meant that audience would recognize pre-existent truths when they saw the films based on their understanding of mythology and sacred texts. Where realistic cinema in the West mimicked what was *apparently* real in the world, this reality was felt only to represent ephemeral or passing truths, because there were sacred truths that were 'truer' than everyday experience. Where to the Lumières and Méliès cinema was an extension of photography, to Phalke it was a recording of sacred performance which was a different kind of mimesis—that of the encounter between the human and the divine.

Phalke saw the Indian purpose of cinema to be different from the way it was regarded in the West, but that is not to imply that he did not credit cinema with other purposes; he also made a few documentaries, including one on the germination of a pea. However, it is important that he saw cinema as the recording of a sacred enactment. This is because even when popular Indian cinema moved out of the genre of the mythological, it continued with the same aesthetics of 'frontality' for decades. Corresponding to this, popular cinema did not deal with ordinary people and everyday action but everything was played out at the heroic level. This means that unlike Hollywood, which told stories derived from the novel as a form, popular Indian cinema, even in the genre of the 'social' (or domestic melodrama set in contemporary times), did not adapt novels but still depended on mythology, although stories were made secular as would be appropriate. Most of popular cinema's motifs in its mature years can, therefore, be traced to the epics and the Puranas.

This crucial aspect of Indian cinema takes it away from Aristotelian mimesis (which tries to replicate the world perceived through the senses) and implies that the notions of realism and expressionism are not applicable to its popular variety. At the same time, cinema is not art for art's sake, but corresponds to mimesis of a special kind posited by classical poetics in India. Although India's poetics may be less pertinent to a study of cinema than its dramaturgy, the traditional view of literature is that it is not subordinate to external reality but actually greater. Where the novel deals with ordinary people engaged in actions credible at the everyday level, mythology deals with larger-than-life situations, with the characters occupying a higher plane than that of everyday life—and popular cinema has tried to imitate only the latter kind of 'truth'. Though the frontal style has been largely abandoned, it still tries to make every situation and every act, whether good or evil, exemplary in some sense. A recent example of this would be Rajkumar Hirani's *3 Idiots* (2009), which is based on a novel by Chetan Bhagat (*Five Point Someone*, 2004). In the film, the ordinary protagonist of the novel is deliberately made larger than life—a technological genius with incredible gifts. This distinction between narratives deriving from mythology and the novel can be used to differentiate between the categories of cinema that have since emerged from India.

Divisions

In its early phases—the silent era to be specific—Indian cinema hardly followed the Phalke mythological model without exception, as available footage that survives today suggests. Apart from Baburao Painter (who made a realistic film about a moneylender, *Savkari Pash* in 1925, of which little remains), there is other evidence of cinema not of the Parsi theatre model. Among these are three films made by the German film-maker Franz Osten—*Prem Sanyas* or *The Light of Asia* (1925), *Shiraz* (1928), and *Prapancha Pash* (1929). These films directed by Osten were produced by Himanshu Rai and scripted by Niranjan Pal, and exhibited abroad with English titles.

It was perhaps only in the sound era, when Parsi theatre could be followed more strictly through the use of songs, that Indian cinema came to acquire its distinctive form. But even after sound and music came into being, there were attempts to step out of the 'heroic' mould and make films about everyday life and common people. There were several important 'reformist' films dealing with social issues—especially those by V. Shantaram, such as *Duniya Na Mane* (1937) in which a young woman is forced into marriage to an old man and resists it—but one cannot say that they break out of the mythical pattern. This aspect will be dealt with separately, but to distinguish it briefly, the novel as a genre deals with individuals while mythology deals with archetypes and emblems representing issues or qualities. The most important versions of *Devdas*— P.C. Barua's films in 1935 and 1936, and Bimal Roy's 1955 version—correspond, arguably, to Devdas as an emblem of male weakness (played by Barua/K.L. Saigal) and as an individual with a psychology (played by Dilip Kumar) unable to conduct himself as he should in his relationship with a woman because of a flaw in his character.

The first sound film to step out of the mythical mould and actually deal with real people, making it a precursor to Satyajit Ray and art cinema, was a film which came out of the Communist-inspired Indian

People's Theatre Association (IPTA). Khwaja Ahmad Abbas's *Dharti Ke Lal* (1946) was jointly written by him and Bijon Bhattacharya, based on the latter's plays and the story '*Annadata*' (1945) by Krishan Chander which dealt with the plight of peasants in the Bengal famine of 1943. One cannot say that the film is entirely successful at representing this, and Ray's *Pather Panchali* (1954) was, therefore, the first genuine success in India in adopting the novelistic mode to cinema.

Although Ray engendered the Indian art film, art cinema as a movement only began around 1970 because of state mediation. The Film Finance Corporation (FFC), which had functioned like any other govern-ment institution, merely supplementing the budgets of successful film-makers, became producer and dis-tributor to another kind of cinema. Where only Ray, who had little support from any institutionalized programme, had represented Indian art cinema and the industry had declared him a cultural icon with-out jeopardizing its own position, art cinema offered competition to mainstream films. The films cited as the first successes of FFC policy are Basu Chatterjee's *Sara Akash* (1969) and Mrinal Sen's *Bhuvan Shome* (1969). Both are models of authenticity and dealt with 'ordinary people' in accordance with the virtues upheld by the policy. They may be taken to be the first films of the art film movement and are exercises in the novelistic mode.

Still, if the arrival of the novelistic form in Indian cinema is responsible for its primary division, we cannot be certain that the division is as clear as one might like it. Ritwik Ghatak is a film-maker whose work does not fit clearly into either category and there are 'fence-sitters' like V. Shantaram and Bimal Roy, and film-makers of middle cinema such as Hrishikesh Mukherjee and Basu Bhattacharya. Art cinema itself often uses the codes of popular cinema, since realistic films dealing with the poor often treat them as emblems of poverty rather than as individuals confronted with economic problems. Another interesting point is that in Kerala (and, perhaps, some other regions), the popular film itself uses the novelistic idiom. The distinction between art and popular cinema, which is so clear in the Hindi language film and many of the regional cinemas, therefore, becomes more nebulous in Malayalam cinema, although this will need a separate investigation. In the global age there has been a further blurring of distinctions, and this will be considered in a later chapter.

Now that a serviceable distinction has been made between narrative modes in the popular film and the art film, associating them with mythology and the novel, respectively, the next step is to make distinctions within the body of popular cinema, and the most helpful way of doing it is to categorize the popular cinemas of India based on the constituencies they address—which depend on language. Art cinema, although made in different languages, emerged from a national initiative promoted by the state, and films still depend on state patronage, as they get most exposure at film festivals. Art cinema may, therefore, be regarded as a pan-Indian category regardless of the language in which it is made.

Popular Cinema and Its Constituencies

Among the popular cinemas of India only the mainstream Hindi film attempts to overlook regional differences and, as a cultural artefact, permeates the farthest corners of the nation. The idiom of Hindi cinema tries to avoid 'local' influences within India to keep its reach widespread. It caters to a 'lowest common denominator' across a larger space and, therefore, eschews much of the vibrancy and the audacity of a localized form of theatre. Even in as sacred a play as *Raja Harishchandra*, when the noble Queen Taramati begs money for the cremation of her dead son, she dances, kicking her heels and swinging her hips. In a religious tale, Sita sings of her tragic plight while casting come-hither glances. Such boldness is unimaginable in the Hindi film when it deals with sacred subject matter. Students of theatre have also commented upon the lewdly non-religious note of 'tamasha' performances while dealing with Krishna and the milkmaids, and such impiety is rare in cinema. The Hindi film is apparently more complaisant and intended to appeal to people spread over a wider territory. This design apparently makes it obligatory for Hindi cinema to avoid any discourses that may cause annoyance. For the same reasons, popular Hindi cinema also keeps its spoken language universally accessible. The Hindi film after 1947, it may be said, therefore, attempts to belong to the 'Indian nation' in a way that other categories of film in India do not and answers more honestly to the description of a national cinema than the pan-Indian art film. It may be noted that autonomous 'national cinemas' in the Third World were often the creations of the Western-educated elite who functioned as prime movers in cultural production. In India, art cinema as a whole has not gained much ground as 'national cinema', while Bollywood's commercial success globally, in the past few decades, has seen it acquiring the respectability that eluded it for quite a while.

The contention that mainstream Hindi cinema is national cinema should not be understood to mean that it is only for consumption by Indians since it has an enormous reach, both within the diaspora and outside. It is similar to Hollywood in that while it upholds values specific to its home territory, these values can still be considered universal in some way by others. This reach of Hindi cinema outside India is shared by some other regional cinemas as well, as, for instance, Tamil and Bhojpuri cinema. Tamil cinema is consumed wherever there is a Tamil diaspora like Malaysia, just as Bhojpuri cinema is reportedly consumed in places like Fiji and Mauritius. In Malaysia, Tamil and Hindi cinema actually compete with each other, as Tamil cinema is popular with ethnic Tamils, while Hindi cinema is consumed more by native Malays. These factors suggest that regional language cinemas also address identities as the Hindi film does and that these identities are determined by the language in which the films are made, although this is not all.

The linguistic reorganization of the states took place in 1956 and territories based on language were created; but this ignored identity issues within the states which gradually came to the fore as the recent division of Andhra Pradesh into the Andhra and Telangana states has proved. How this further division of language identity influences regional language cinema is difficult to establish, but there is little doubt that it does. If Telugu cinema has largely been an Andhra cinema, Kannada cinema addressed the people of the princely state of Mysore ruled over by the maharaja. After the Kannada-speaking areas from the Madras Presidency, Bombay Presidency, Nizam's Hyderabad, as well as Coorg (now Kodagu) became part of Greater Mysore (renamed Karnataka in 1974), Kannada cinema apparently continued to address the same territories that once constituted the princely state of Mysore. This is suggested by the kind of Kannada employed as well as the choice of the protagonists, who are almost never from the non-Mysore regions of Karnataka like Gulbarga, Mangalore, etc. Hindi cinema as a body itself includes 'B' category films constituted by cheap horror and action films which does well in the small towns of the Hindi belt and in some parts of the metropolises. There is justification to describe this cinema as 'regional Hindi cinema'.

This division of Indian cinema into regional cinemas actually divides cinema in terms of the subjects chosen and their treatment, implying that there is much more than language which is at stake. To only hint at the variety available in the popular cinemas: an archetypal plot from a recent, successful, mainstream Hindi film around 2010 revolves around young people with personal aspirations travelling abroad in Europe, living the lifestyles of the rich, and being steeped in a life of consumption and discovering genuine love (*Zindagi Na Milegi Dobara*, or *ZNMD*, 2011). The archetypal plot of the successful Kannada blockbuster roughly contemporary to it (*Duniya*, 2007) revolves around a young migrant from rural Karnataka coming to Bengaluru, not finding quarters and sleeping on the pavement, eating in the cheapest eateries in the squalid parts of the city, becoming embroiled in gangland disputes, and rising to the stature of a feared leader, however, being liquidated by a low-ranking policeman in an encounter before the love he has found can come to fruition. As if corresponding to these diverse scenarios, there are enormous differences in the admission prices paid by spectators in movie halls as well. While audiences from the metropolises pay anywhere up to Rs 500 (or more) for a ticket in a multiplex, the average ticket price is only around Rs 35 across the rest of India, suggesting that the cost of admission in a majority of places could be as low as Rs 20. One could gather from this that cinema in India reaches a whole range of spectators, and that the stark economic differences that India is known for shows in the spectator profiles as well. The mainstream Hindi film lies somewhere within this range, but it would not be accurate to describe either its concerns or its audiences as constituted homogeneously.

The Constitution of the Book

'Bollywood' is a recent term that should not, in all fairness, be applied to *all of* popular Hindi cinema, but it is nonetheless an effective sign if only to evoke it. Producing a comprehensive volume on Indian popular cinema is perhaps an impossible task, but a short introduction restricted to mainstream Hindi cinema is more easily done. A great deal of work has been done by academics, many of whom have either got their doctorates from American universities or are working there. Much of this work, however, has not addressed the curiosity of the intelligent filmgoing public and its interest has remained confined to academia. Different kinds of meanings can be constructed from Hindi cinema, and the earliest serious writing tried to apply either psychoanalysis or procedures derived from cultural studies to examine its ideology. They were not actively engaged in understanding the attractions of Hindi cinema for its spectators. This introduction is primarily interested in the effect of Hindi cinema upon its audiences and will, therefore, not dwell overly on the formulations of these scholars and theorists. This is not to say that the meanings it constructs from Hindi cinema will be the most obvious ones, as audiences could also respond subliminally to visual stimuli and may not be in a position to entirely articulate the effect that a film has on them. A film addresses an audience that has social experiences in common and the limits placed on the experiences will also tend to exclude others from its reach. This means that many aspects of a Hindi film that are self-evident to Indians may not be absorbed readily by cultural outsiders. The exceptional nature of India's artistic/aesthetic tradition and cultural/political history are broadly held as the reason for Bollywood triumphing on its own turf when other, better established, cinemas have fallen under the global onslaught of Hollywood.

The thrust of this book is, therefore, towards comprehending this 'exceptionality'. In accordance with this aim, the remainder of the book is divided into four chapters.

Chapter 1, 'The Historical Trajectory of the Hindi Film Narrative', will look largely at changing film motifs in the light of unfolding history, the plot devices that became popular in certain periods, and their significance. The chapter will divide Hindi cinema into various eras and examine each one of these: pre-Independence cinema, including the reformist films of the 1930s and the 1940s; post-Independence Nehruvian-era cinema ending around 1962 with the Sino-Indian War; the arrival of escapist cinema in the 1960s; cinema under Indira Gandhi, including 'middle cinema' beginning with the art film movement; cinema in the remaining years of the Nehruvian socialist period; and cinema after the liberalization of 1991.

Chapter 2, 'The Grammar and Aesthetics of Popular Hindi Cinema', will examine key aspects of the mainstream Hindi film that set it apart, chiefly its defining of space and time, causality, ethical discourse, and moral instruction. The chapter will also deal with gender and the meaning of romance, melodrama and its significance, the proliferation of types, the use of the passive voice, point-of-view and the omniscient eye, and the dominant ideology. Parallels will be drawn with literature and the other arts including dramatic performance.

Chapter 3, 'The Production and Distribution of Hindi Films', will give an account of the production apparatus in place and the system used for the distribution of Hindi cinema in India as well as the economics of film production today.

Chapter 4, 'Global Bollywood', will look at the changing shape of Hindi cinema after it became a global brand called 'Bollywood' in the new millennium. It will speculate about the future of Hindi cinema, with special reference to whether it can retain its place as a national cinema as it has been.

Style and Tenor

A regrettable feature of film practice in India has been the absence of codification of film form and convention. This has been so severe that even people belonging to families that have worked for generations in the film industry have been unable to get the benefits of accumulated experience. The state of affairs is partly blamed on the non-availability of much lucid and yet penetrating documentation of cinematic mores in India. This may also be responsible for a degree of instability in film convention and grammar, since many film-makers have not been educated in the past of their own cinema and work as if by instinct; this book, therefore, proposes to fill a much needed gap. It hopes to provide a quick and lucid look at important aspects of Hindi cinema that interest film students who take its achievements as artistic endeavour seriously, and initiate them into its methods. However, while avoiding jargon assiduously, it still demands attentive reading since the Hindi film raises intellectual issues that no introduction can neglect to address. An effort has been made to embrace complex issues and do so to facilitate a quick grasp of the subject. Lastly, while there will be some paraphrasing of film stories, the films are not always described in such a way as will be familiar to readers, as the purpose will be to understand them only in specific contexts.

1

The Historical Trajectory of the Hindi Film Narrative

Reformism and Pre-Independence Cinema

Since the Introduction introduced D.G. Phalke and conveyed a sense of silent cinema, this chapter will identify and explore the narrative motifs in Hindi cinema before 1947. It has been acknowledged that— much more than in any other cinema outside India— the spectator's response to Hindi cinema concentrates upon the story. Songs, although extremely pertinent, are nonetheless enjoyed independently and survive long after the films are forgotten, which is not true of the Hollywood musical. There is hence some justification in charting Hindi cinema's historical trajectory in terms of narrative strategies and motifs. Songs, perhaps, need to be accommodated within a separate history.

The 'primitive period' in American cinema is considered to have concluded in 1908; and if the stability of film motifs is taken as an indication, the motifs of Hindi cinema began to show some degree of stability around 1930, almost at the same time as the arrival of sound, with Ardeshir Irani's *Alam Ara* (1931). It should, however, be noted that wisdom on Hindi cinema's early past is largely based on hearsay since much film material is lost, and this proposition about the stability of narrative motifs is based on the films' actual availability in their entirety. The two complete films available at the National Film Archive of India in Pune are both historical films from the Agarwal stable—*Diler Jigar* (aka *Gallant Hearts*) and *Ghulami Nu Pattan* (aka *The Fall of Slavery*), both made in 1931. The films feature strong women characters, with *Diler Jigar* introducing a masked female vigilante, prefiguring Fearless Nadia in Homi Wadia's *Hunterwali* (1935). The films made by Franz Osten in the 1920s, mentioned in the Introduction, are omitted from consideration here since they are 'orientalist' ventures which do not reflect on later Indian cinema.

As already suggested, the film form transformed considerably after the arrival of sound (and music), but I will deal with form and syntax separately in the next chapter. The most important cinema produced before 1947, largely belonging to a genre called the 'reformist social', can be understood in relation to the reform movements of the nineteenth century, regarded as having been initiated by the Christian missions, but tailored subsequently by the nationalist Indian middle class. The key components of this reformist initiative would include the founding of the Brahmo Samaj by Raja Rammohun Roy, the work of religious and social reformers like Swami Vivekananda, Dayananda Saraswati, and Iswarchandra Vidyasagar, and the literary output of writers like Bankim Chandra Chatterjee, Rabindranath Tagore, Sarat Chandra Chatterjee, Marathi novelist Hari Narayan Apte, and Munshi Premchand, a novelist who wrote in Hindi as well as Urdu. Among the aspects of reform resulting from the movement were the abolition of abhorrent institutions like sati, attempts to give Hinduism the appearance of a unified religion by invoking the Vedas and the Upanishads, and the according of prominence to Sankaracharya's monism (Advaita) within the religion.

It has been surmised that an attempt was made to project back into history a golden age of Hinduism which was an ancient version of the West. The literature of the period was also preoccupied with 'Christianizing' Hinduism; Bankim Chandra's version of Krishna tried to make the god more acceptable to non-Hindus, reducing his androgynous characteristics and making him a less 'pagan' deity. It has also been argued that an attempt was made to erect a patriarchal godhead like the Judeo-Christian one, instead of the matriarchal one. Perhaps, as a compensating process, this led to a greater social role for women. All these aspects of reform could not have come about if there had not been a sense of traditional Hinduism—with its magical and irrational elements—not measuring up morally to the religion of the colonizers, and 'reformism' may be regarded as nationalism's way of overcoming this sense of inadequacy. It is as a consequence of the reformist endeavour that films of the 1930s and the early 1940s are most fruitfully regarded. *Amritmanthan* (1934) is about the elimination of a cult engaged in human sacrifices, *Chandidas* (1932) and *Achhut Kanya* (1936) are about caste discrimination, *Duniya Na Mane* is about a young woman forced into marriage to an elderly widower but who resists him, *Samaj Ki Bhool* (1934) is about the widow's right to remarry, *President* (1937) is about the exploitation of labour in industry, and *Dharti Mata* (1938) advocates the technological transformation of the agrarian sector. Reform and cinema revolved around the spaces in which the colonial interface was strongest, that is, the Presidency towns, and many of the best writers also worked in cinema for a while. Munshi Premchand, a doyen of reformist Hindi literature from Varanasi, spent the last portion of his life in Bombay (now Mumbai) where he tried to work in the film industry.

Strong Woman, Weak Man

The different orderings of sexuality by colonial culture and traditional Hinduism, respectively, are of specific significance in the period of reform. As Ashis Nandy notes, colonial culture assumed that manliness (*purusatva*) was superior to womanliness (*naritva*) which was itself superior to femininity in man (*klibatva*), while saintliness, highly regarded in Hindu belief, also included femininity-in-masculinity as an associated quality. It may be difficult to trace the logical process here, but

there was an association of the colonizers with masculinity and the colonized with femininity, which may
be interpreted as a 'crisis of masculinity', and is strongly
expressed in Hindi cinema until the early 1940s. This
shows itself in the motif of the weak man and the strong
woman in films as different as P.C. Barua's *Devdas*
(1935), Damle and Fattelal's *Sant Tukaram* (1936),
and Homi Wadia's *Hunterwali*, which are a 'social', a
mythological, and an action film, respectively. Devdas's
weakness resulting from his domination by his father
in Barua's version emerges as a failure of masculinity,
while the notion is treated quite differently in *Sant
Tukaram* in which weak masculinity takes the shape
of klibatva; the saint, because of his otherworldliness,
needs his strong wife to attend to the family. Some other
films showing the motif of the strong woman include
V. Shantaram's *Duniya Na Mane* and *Aadmi* (1939),
Mehboob Khan's *Aurat* (1940), which was later remade
as *Mother India* (1956), N.R. Acharya's *Azad* (1940),
Franz Osten's *Durga* (1939), and Gyan Mukherjee's
Jhoola (1931). Many of these films have the young
Ashok Kumar, who has an androgynous presence, as
the protagonist. The motif of the strong woman and the
weak man leaves Hindi cinema abruptly around 1942

with there being no further female vigilante or saint films after that, of which there had been several earlier. An explanation is the Japanese invasion of Burma (now Myanmar) and the annexation of Singapore, when British masculinity came into question. The nationalist mood was also upbeat; Gandhi dismissed the offers made by the Cripps Mission as a 'cheque on a failing bank' and the Quit India Movement was launched. Interestingly, there are two films from 1943, Mehboob Khan's *Taqdeer* (1943) and Gyan Mukherjee's *Kismet* (1943) in which a son breaks with his domineering father. In *Taqdeer*, his adoptive mother who has lost her mind and taken him for a girl, regains her sanity and acknowledges him as masculine. Ashok Kumar's career as hero also concludes around this time and the roles he takes up thereafter are different.

Anticipating Independence and Partition

When independence began to be anticipated after 1943, the Muslim question became gradually more important in India, and this led to Indian cinema explicitly affirming the Muslim ruler's place in India's tradition. The most important films to perform the function are *Tansen* (1943), *Humayun* (1945), and *Shahjehan* (1946). It is acknowledged that the historical film provides a rich source of knowledge into the way a society reconstructs its self-image by projecting into the past the imperatives of the present, and, consequently, operates on a basic past-present duality. These three films are nominally about the past, but they also pose the historical question of the Muslims' position in India. In *Humayun*, Babar's army overruns a Hindu kingdom but he generously installs the Rajput princess as monarch and becomes a 'father' to her. Humayun, therefore, becomes her 'brother', although the Princess' fiancé, the Rajput prince Randhir swears vengeance, as Humayun caused his father's death. Babar also asserts that he is not a plunderer and that he is in Hindustan to stay on, and Humayun also declares to Randhir (while refusing to go into battle) that he will never leave.

Loyalty to the nation-to-be is a key motif carried forward outside the historical film as well. Mehboob Khan is a director of great importance in this period and his *Anmol Ghadi* (1946) is one of the most interesting of Hindi films. In this film, a poor boy and a rich girl love each other in childhood, but her father, who disapproves of the relationship, takes her away to the city. The boy is brought up by his widowed mother, who works to provide him with food and education. When he becomes an adult, the boy follows the girl to the city to pursue their love, ignoring his mother's remonstrations that the rich and the poor cannot come together since they have their own preoccupations. The mother ages and sickens, but the young man neglects her in pursuit of his love, until the girl reveals that she cannot marry him and marries his rich friend instead. When his mother dies uncared for, he cremates her and wonders (through a song) who one's kin really are.

Anmol Ghadi may be the first to introduce the figure of the sacred mother, and 'mother-as-bread-provider' (which is given emphasis) as a convenient symbol for the land. One is, therefore, tempted to interpret the film as allegory. The message of the film then becomes 'Do not desert your land to follow the rich'. Mehboob and the scriptwriter Aghajani Kashmeri were both progressive Muslims apprehensive about the imminent Partition, and the film can be read as an entreaty to fellow Muslims to not to leave their land. The Muslim League was dominated by the rich, but had a following of poor people, and this may explain the motif. Not much should be made of the characters being Hindu,

9

because, to Mehboob Khan, Muslims were 'people' and not 'Muslims'. By the conventions of the Hindi film, a Hindu is a 'person' and not someone specifically of the religion, and this will be elaborated upon in the next chapter. The figure of the sacred mother appears frequently in Hindi cinema after 1947 in various capacities, because of the arrival of the nation as an object of loyalty. This allegorical aspect of popular cinema follows from films having to address an audience with shared social experience, appealing to those aspects held in common with a national community. Frederic Jameson has argued that since 'private life' has not developed in the Third World as in the developed countries, all stories have public connotations and, wittingly or unwittingly, they become allegories of the nation. An allegory (like John Bunyan's 1678 work *The Pilgrim's Progress*) deliberately represents abstract notions though concrete characters and events, but Jameson suggests that it could also be unintentional.

Melodrama, Loyalty, and Conflict

The domestic melodrama (or the 'reformist social') originating in the colonial period has already been discussed. While the domestic melodrama is only one category in the 1930s and the early 1940s, the mythological being the other, the social begins to dominate Hindi cinema after 1947. Post-Independence melodrama may be understood as a continuation of the socials of the earlier period, but there are nonetheless crucial differences. Critics have noted that Independence acquires figurability in many films after 1947, and the chief reason is the arrival of loyalty towards an individual or a community as a strong motif, as in *Anmol Ghadi*. Where people were 'good' and 'bad' earlier, we have a new entity transcending this polarity: the male protagonist of Mehboob's film is 'good' but nonetheless neglects the mother who did much for him. It is this loyalty towards the independent nation that translates into an 'Oedipal conflict'—as in Raj Kapoor's *Awaara* (1951)—the Freudian motif is not in evidence before the independent nation enters the narrative. This loyalty which is tested can also be towards a friend (denoted as *dosti* and seen later in *Naya Daur*, 1957). Loyalty towards the community is exhibited most famously in Mehboob's *Mother India*, when the mother sacrifices her rebellious son for going against the law of the community. Unlike in *Aurat*, of which it is a remake, the mother in *Mother India* is a matriarch and mother figure to the community; also, the son in this film is a rebel rather than a criminal.

If loyalty is brought into focus after 1947, there is also a new admission of responsibility through the notion of conflict between warring classes and between different attitudes towards the poor and the marginalized. Frequently, it shows itself in the class differences between the hero and heroine becoming insurmountable, as shown in *Bawre Nain* (1950) and *Babul* (1950). In *Anokhi Ada* (1948), an urbane young man who wears a rose in his buttonhole and loves children takes care of an orphan girl and her brother, a motif that may have come about with the death of the Father of the Nation and the consequent feeling that the 'orphaned' Indians became the responsibility of Pandit Nehru (whose sartorial habits included the rose in the buttonhole). These films are not alike but still find the means to introduce the same motifs within different generic structures. For instance, in Kamal Amrohi's *Mahal* (1949), the notion of two women from different classes fighting for the same man occurs in a ghostly tale. A key presence in many of these films is Dilip Kumar, whose performances in *Babul* and

12

Jogan (1950) are endowed with an existential freedom uncharacteristic of the Hindi film; it is as though the male protagonist is exercising moral choices that are not typical of film heroes, who were, and have been, frozen as types. One could argue that Independence gave Indians the abrupt sense of becoming responsible for themselves and revealed itself thus in cinema.

The Perils and Attractions of Modernity

A key notion in the years after Independence and persisting until the early 1960s is that of modernity, viewed as a threat earlier, but which gradually comes to be accepted. One of the first of the films is Mehboob Khan's *Andaz* (1949) which stars Nargis as the heroine and both Dilip Kumar and Raj Kapoor as her male counterparts. In this film, the heroine is motherless and spoilt by her millionaire father and her 'modern' ways are interpreted as 'love' by one of the men although she is already engaged to the other, and this leads to tragedy. Soon, however, Hindi cinema admits the attractions of modernity, and we find modernity being classified separately as good (as symbolized by the doctor) and bad (as represented by the nightclub and

Western dance) as instantiated in Guru Dutt's *Baazi* (1951). In this film a club dancer and a lady doctor vie for the hero (Dev Anand). If Dilip Kumar's early roles betoken 'independence' because of the existential freedom they assume, Dev Anand emblemized the perils of modernity in the Nehruvian era. He is usually amoral and engaged in some nefarious activity or other: as a gambler in *Baazi*, a smuggler in Guru Dutt's *Jaal* (1952), black-marketeer of film tickets in *Kala Bazaar* (1960). He is also seen frequently in disguise pretending to belong to a social class other than his own. It was this amoral persona of Dev Anand that was later harnessed effectively in Vijay Anand's *Guide* (1965), in which the hero forges a signature and goes to prison. *Guide* is based on a novel by R.K. Narayan, but it is adapted as a mainstream Hindi film with its action and characters in the mythical-heroic mould.

Baazi is an important film in many ways, among which an important reason is that it gives a key role to the policeman, who becomes the moral arbiter. The policeman and the judge who could be mocked in the colonial era (as in *Taqdeer*) assume a new gravity after 1947, implying the sanctity of state authority, which becomes a moral presence. The courtroom becomes

14

the space in which the truth cannot be denied, and surrendering to the police or the court also becomes an admission of moral guilt as in Zia Sarhadi's *Footpath* (1953) and Ramesh Saigal's *Phir Subha Hogi* (1958), based on Fyodor Dostoyevsky's *Crime and Punishment*. But to show that the state is itself subject to interrogation, cinema has the motif of the judge or the policeman himself standing trial, as in Raj Kapoor's *Awaara* (1951), Raj Khosla's *CID* (1956), and Yash Chopra's *Dhool Ka Phool* (1959). The state itself being strictly impartial is suggested by K. Asif's *Mughal-e-Azam* (1960) in which the emperor Akbar punishes his own son for the misdemeanour of being involved in the wrong kind of romance.

Another motif of importance in the later part of the 1950s is that of the city which is equated with Nehruvian modernity. The city is associated with the urban criminal, as in Guru Dutt's *Aar Paar* (1954) and Shakti Samantha's *Howrah Bridge* (1958); it is both the site of social optimism as in *Aar Paar* and of deep pessimism as in *Pyasa* (1957) and as can be seen in Raj Kapoor's *Shri 420* (1955). As if to mirror the ambivalence with which the Nehruvian city was viewed, the street lamp—which emphasizes the light it emits and the darkness outside—is a frequent emblem found on film posters. The idea of 'national construction' is optimistically connoted with frequent depictions of irrigation channels, as in *Mother India*, dams, and the dam-construction engineer, as in Raj Kapoor's *Aah* (1953) and Shakti Samantha's *Insan Jaag Utha* (1959), but the city and its entrepreneurs are sometimes also seen with luddite alarm, as in B.R. Chopra's *Naya Daur*, in which an ebullient rustic (Dilip Kumar) races his tonga with a bus as part of a challenge with a crooked city businessman (Jeevan).

The description of optimism with regard to the 'modern' in Indian cinema will be incomplete if we do not take into account the portrayal of women, and Nargis is really the woman star of the 1950s. Her portrayals are always that of the strong woman, but one could also say that unlike in the early 1940s, the strong woman also submits to her social role, and Nargis's performances opposite Raj Kapoor are most typical of these. There is nonetheless another aspect to these films, because women in these films are not sexual objects but exhibit desire. This can be seen not only in *Awaara* and *Shri 420* but in *Dhool Ka Phool*, starring Mala Sinha. Rajendra Kumar, who plays the male lead, was often cast in the role of the man desired by women.

Because of the importance given to modernity and (thus its emblem) the city in the 1950s, agrarian issues are not so much in evidence, although land-reform-related issues are—through the figure of the wicked moneylender and the zamindar which is dealt with occasionally. This was the period in which the Communist-inspired Telangana uprising was going on, and *Mother India* can be read as an allegory of the mother-as-nation being willing to punish her favourite sons if they did not respect the laws of the land. In *Ganga Jumna* (1961), Nitin Bose's later film, the punishment betokened in *Mother India* becomes blunter, when the brother who is also a police officer guns down his rebellious sibling and marries the daughter of the rapacious zamindar—who is herself blameless. One even detects in this motif a new alignment between state authority and feudal power.

Escapist Cinema

The period of nationalistic optimism for Hindi cinema ends abruptly with the debacle of the Sino-Indian War of 1962. A charge once made against Hindi cinema is that it was escapist, and if a cause is to be identified, it is this military defeat, which reveals itself in various ways. The films of the 1950s take their social responsibilities very seriously. Since the city was a site of optimism in the 1950s, the locales after 1962 shift to hill stations and picturesque spots, beginning with Raj Kapoor's *Sangam* (1964), set at the time of war, and there are a number of films which also venture abroad. To show how modernity itself becomes a non-issue after 1962, if good and bad modernity were once represented by the doctor and Western dancing, respectively, *Woh Kaun Thi* (1964), which is set in a hill station, has a Western dance routine in which doctors and nurses participate together. Where earlier films had convoluted resolutions because the nation had to be implicated in them, arbitrary villains are introduced along with noisy fight sequences, and resolutions are affected anyhow. Films are often constructed around finding brides, as in *Kashmir Ki Kali* (1963) and family reunions as in *Waqt* (1965), in which resolutions only fulfil the closure imperative. Despite a few exceptions, like H.S. Rawail's *Mere Mehboob* (1963), Bimal Roy's *Bandini* (1963), and Vijay Anand's *Guide* (1965), the cinematic achievements of the period are meagre. Especially favoured are glitzy devices derived from Bond films like sliding doors and villains in disguise, as in the crime/ spy thrillers exemplified by *Jewel Thief* (1967) and *Farz* (1967). Rajendra Kumar and Jeetendra are the most successful male stars in the cinema of this period.

In 1965, India fought a more successful war against Pakistan, and this brings some thematic seriousness to cinema. The high point was reached in Manoj Kumar's *Upkaar* (1967), which deals with Pakistan both as actual military adversary and in an allegory. The central story about two brothers quarrelling and having to divide the family land (also echoed in Raj Khosla's *Do Raaste*, 1969) is evidently the story of Partition retold. An agrarian motif is also seen in films such as *Upkaar*, which is about a progressive farmer and his tussle with a trader. This can be related to the rising power of farmers in the 1960s with the Green Revolution, which owed its success to large investments in irriga-tion by the state in the 1950s, as in Punjab. But Hindi cinema witnesses a greater transformation with the rise of Indira Gandhi.

Mrs Gandhi enters Hindi cinema innocuously through her person and there are two films which may be taken to allegorize her changing position. The first one, *Padosan* (1968), a hilarious comedy, introduces a cunning south Indian (Mehmood) who manipulates a north Indian woman to keep her from another north Indian (Sunil Dutt) who loves her, until the latter's friends come to his assistance and form a north-Indian fraternity to oust the south-Indian fraternity. This film was made in the period when Mrs Gandhi was prime minister, but was seen to be manipulated by the group within the Congress called the 'Syndicate' dominated by south Indians such as Kamaraj from Tamil Nadu and S. Nijalingappa from Karnataka, both bald and accustomed to wearing dhotis as the character played by Mehmood also was! The second film *Aradhana* (1969) was made after Mrs Gandhi emerged triumphant within the Congress and can be read as a mythical account of a lonely woman who overcomes great odds. Interestingly, the lonely woman has a son who is a pilot, albeit in the Indian Air Force. The husband who sired this son exists only in a distant past and little is publicly known about her marriage. These aspects find correspondence in the way Mrs Gandhi was perceived—with a pilot son Rajiv and as the widow of Feroze Gandhi, about whom little was known.

The Indira Gandhi Era

As a broad creed, Nehruvian socialism still remains in evidence in the 1960s, in the idea of the poor as equals of the rich; but the special privileging of poverty as an issue is generally absent from Hindi cinema of this period, which also loses interest in the nation-building issues dominating it in the 1950s. This alters in the 1970s, with Mrs Gandhi's populism and the associated rhetoric energizing the public space.

The 1970s begins with the rise of Rajesh Khanna, a male star who lacked the threatening quality associated with male power, and who may even be regarded as having been objectified as a female sex symbol might be. It is difficult to explain his fame as a historical phenomenon, but his passive appeal marks the transition between escapism and the new kind of political rhetoric flooding the public space, and he often takes the place of a catalyst for change: doing little himself but nonetheless causing a transformation in the lives of others. A frequent ploy is the goodness of the character played by him sparking off a crisis and enabling a resolution as in *Anand* (1971), in which people are brought together by their newly found ability to admit their true feelings, and in *Bawarchi* (1972), where his presence helps bring order to a dysfunctional family.

Among Mrs Gandhi's earliest political moves is her courting the small bourgeoisie while acting against the monopoly houses. The film to register this is Raj Kapoor's *Bobby* (1973), in which a small businessman (Premnath) lashes out against the industrialist (Pran) who considers himself higher in status and will not permit his son (Rishi Kapoor) to marry the former's daughter (Dimple Kapadia). Another motif seen at this time was that of the committed judiciary, which would redefine legality to admit the marginalized into the mainstream. The marginalized are often represented in the Hindi films of the time as good-hearted petty criminals and there are key films in which the state (as represented by the police officer) enlists petty thieves/bootleggers to fight greater evils, as in *Zanjeer* (1973) and *Sholay* (1975). Another aspect of Mrs Gandhi's rhetoric was its anti-Western bias and this often finds bizarre representation with Western decadence and drugs as shown in *Purab Aur Paschim* (1970) and *Hare Rama Hare Krishna* (1971) and the blond-haired foreign smuggler flying temple idols out of India as in *Yaadon Ki Baraat* (1973). Amitabh Bachchan's

'Angry Young Man' acts from *Deewar* (1975), *Muqaddar Ka Sikandar* (1978), *Trishul* (1978), *Shakti* (1982), and *Agneepath* (1990) are perhaps the most conspicuous motifs from the period. Political rhetoric in the period played up social injustice as a cause of disaffection, and the Angry Young Man is someone who has been wronged by such injustice and carries its scars, which manifest themselves in a life of illegality, although with honour.

An important development in the period was the impetus given to art cinema (dealt with previously), which also engendered a 'middle cinema' represented by directors like Basu Chatterjee (*Rajnigandha*, 1974) and Hrishikesh Mukherjee (*Namak Haraam*, 1973), who made films which deal with individuals rather than types, but also took up social issues seriously. Mukherjee's *Abhimaan* (1973) is about the career rivalry between singers married to each other; this is something that mainstream cinema would not have tackled because it allows a new psychological complexity not characteristic of mythology, but of the novel.

Mrs Gandhi's rule seems momentous, but her heady period lasted barely a few years because she imposed Emergency in 1975 to prevent being unseated. She was often compared to Goddess Shakti at the time and one of India's most famous painters, M.F. Hussain, even portrayed her as such. This was a black period for cinema, especially for the Hindi belt, and a super hit of 1975, a mythological 'B' film *Jai Santoshi Maa* (1975) deals with a good woman who triumphs over three fearsome Shakti goddesses through her saintliness. The most famous villain in Hindi film history, Gabbar Singh (Amjad Khan) of Ramesh Sippy's *Sholay*, may also be a depiction of state authoritarianism since he is a whimsical tyrant who dresses in khaki. One of his creators, Javed Akhtar, also describes Gabbar's peculiarity in an interview as owing to the impersonality of his tyranny, that is, Gabbar expressing concern for the punishment he is himself going to administer to an underling.

Hindi cinema of the 1970s gradually grows grotesque in shape, arguably because of the radical rhetoric in the public space in the absence of political faith. With the surfeit of political optimism and the marking out of social enemies as embodied in smugglers (targeted under the Conservation of Foreign Exchange and Prevention of Smuggling Activities Act) and other practitioners of evil (often played by Ajit), it begins to parody itself. The high point of this baroque phase is reached in Manmohan Desai's *Amar Akbar Anthony* (1977), which plays hilariously with every motif of the period: children separated at birth and brought up in different religions, the petty criminal joining hands with the law, the honest man driven to crime by poverty, religious faith providing miracles, identical twins who follow different moral trajectories (scientist and arch-criminal), and the stereotypical sacred mother (Nirupa Roy) separated from her caring husband and children but reunited in the end. Mrs Gandhi lost power in 1977; the three years in which the Janata alliance ruled with different prime ministers were uneventful for Hindi cinema, which produced little of interest. When Mrs Gandhi won the mid-term elections in 1980, her second stint produced entirely different results.

A Violent Decade

According to political scientists, the 1980s were a period in which 'divisive forces' had gained impetus within the Indian polity because of regional demands. If the last years of the Janata Party rule saw the squabbling between constituents (with regional loyalties) weaken-ing the traditionally strong centre, Indira Gandhi also ruled more tentatively in her second reign. One of Mrs Gandhi's manoeuvres had been the initial encouragement of a young Sikh religious preacher named Jarnail Singh Bhindranwale as part of an effort to weaken the faction-ridden Akali Dal, which had participated in the Janata coalition. But when she returned to power in 1980, she assumed he was expendable and chose to disregard him after he had campaigned for the Congress. Bhindranwale had, however, captured the imagination of many a Sikh youth by now, and encouraged them to question the authority of the Indian state and speak the language of secession. The centre was also beset by conflicting regional demands: the states that had done well like Punjab sought greater autonomy, while others like Assam, which believed they had been neglected, demanded a larger share in central revenue. One of the results of this vote-bank politics (when group identities are actively promoted for short-term electoral gain) was that the groups began to gradually assert themselves. Regional politics also came forcefully alive, and differently from in the 1950s. The claims of regional autonomy then faced were reactions to the legacies of colonial rule, which had created administrative territories containing linguistic groups that had become discontented. The regional demands of the 1980s, in contrast, were directed against the centre, which had meddled in regional affairs, frequently invoking 'the President's rule' and undermining federalism.

Films from the 1980s are striking in their depiction of onscreen violence. *Sholay* provides the most striking example of screen violence before 1980 but the films of the 1980s are different from Ramesh Sippy's film. Typical examples from this decade are B.R. Chopra's *Insaaf Ka Tarazu* (1980); N. Chandra's *Ankush* (1985), *Pratighaat* (1987), and *Tezaab* (1988), Mukul S. Anand's *Agneepath*, two 'youth' films such as K. Balachander's *Ek Duuje Ke Liye* (1982) and Mansoor Khan's *Qayamat Se Qayamat Tak* (*QSQT*, 1988), Rahul Rawail's *Arjun* (1985), and Raj Kumar Santoshi's *Ghayal* (1990). The violence in *Sholay*, although dramatic, is 'cleaner' inasmuch as it is set in rustic spaces rather than in the confusing ambience of the contemporary city as the films of this decade usually are. Interestingly enough, the city made a departure from popular cinema after 1962, but reappeared in the 1970s, although not with the same significance. In films like *Deewar* and *Trishul*, the migrant hero makes the city his home and rises in it through dubious or unlawful means. Where the city of the 1950s was a space marked out for the encounter with modernity, these later films regard it mainly as the emblem of opportunity. The city is nominally portrayed as 'corrupting', but material advancement in it is made so enticing that the attractions override any discourse about its evils. While we can associate this portrayal with the promise of upward mobility in Mrs Gandhi's first period as prime minister, the films of the 1980s offer another kind of discourse. The motifs dominating the films of this decade and accounting for much of the violence are classifiable as pertaining to rape and 'feminine dishonour', gang rivalries and urban criminals, caste violence, and regional antagonisms. Many films work with more than one of these motifs and an aspect that also connects them is their portrayal of the police and or the judiciary as weak.

Insaaf Ka Tarazu begins with a sequence in which an unknown woman is being raped by an unknown assailant until a protector arrives and kills him. The very next scene occurs in court, where a decorated army officer (Dharmendra) is being tried for murder. The officer declares that he has killed in the service of the nation before, and that he will kill again to save a woman's honour, because a woman's honour is as sacred as that of the motherland. The film invites us to read the act of dishonouring women as a metaphor; this, however, does not mean that it does not use rape exploitatively. This motif occurs frequently and goes along with the notion of regional identity as in *Ankush*, in which Marathi speakers from Bombay are oppressed by north Indians with more economic power. The same motif is also in evidence in *Ek Duuje Ke Liye*, in which romance between a south-Indian boy and a north-Indian girl faces violent obstacles, until the lovers are killed. Caste features prominently in *QSQT*, although it is not inter-caste antagonism as much as violent rivalry between families within the same Kshatriya caste in which young lovers pay the price as in *Ek Duuje Ke Liye*. Among the more interesting films of the period are J.P. Dutta's *Ghulami* (1985), *Yateem* (1988), *Batwara* (1989), and *Hathyar* (1989), about the Kshatriya propensity for violence without ethics being considered. In *Batwara*, a thakur (Kshatriya) policeman (Amrish Puri) declares that he is a thakur first and a policeman only afterwards, an indication of how the polity in India was divided along caste and regional lines. Another figure to gain prominence is the gangster of whom the police are frightened (*Tezaab*, *Agneepath*).

In N. Chandra's *Pratighaat*, a judge shuts his window hastily when a woman is paraded naked in the street by a gang of hoodlums; cinema had evidently come some way since the 1950s, when judges and policemen were figures of moral authority.

Mrs Gandhi was assassinated by her Sikh bodyguards in November 1984 as revenge for Operation Blue Star (June 1984), in which the Indian military attacked the Golden Temple in Amritsar to capture the militants holed up inside. The number of civilian casualties was estimated at around 500, with Bhindranwale himself among them. Mrs Gandhi's death was followed by the anti-Sikh riots in Delhi, in which nearly 3,000 Sikhs were killed. None of these events are reflected in Hindi cinema, and a reason may be (as will be elaborated upon later) that the motifs of Hindi cinema narrativize expectations rather than completed happenings. But the motif of a young Sikh in an anti-terrorist squad sacrificing himself for the motherland is found in Subhash Ghai's *Karma* (1986). A major turning point for Hindi cinema was the economic liberalization of 1991, but it took three years for its effects to be felt. In the early 1990s, cinema continues to exhibit the motifs of the 1980s, as in films like Rajkumar

Santoshi's *Damini* (1993), a powerful story of rape and its consequences.

Teleological Shift for the Nation

An extremely influential development in Indian economic history was the extensive economic reforms proposed in June 1991 and February 1992 by the Narasimha Rao government. Previous governments (such as Rajiv Gandhi's in the later part of the 1990s) had already made tentative moves towards deregulation, but the initiatives of 1991–2 were dictated by wider international developments. The collapse of the Soviet Union and the socialist economies had, apart from disrupting a convenient barter system for Indian goods, also removed the only alternative model to the capitalist market. There could no longer be significant opposition within India for a comprehensive loosening of state control over the economy, and business and industrial interests, therefore, found new political allies. Prime Minister P.V. Narasimha Rao and Finance Minister Manmohan Singh were not politicians with strong constituencies, but their perceived 'weakness' actually worked in their favour. The killing of

Rajiv Gandhi in 1991 left politics a 'level playing field' in India. A vulnerable government with few economic options initiated the economic reforms of 1991–2, but the 'inevitability' of the reforms was widely accepted; the perception that the government was 'helpless' actually lent the reforms legitimacy. In effect, therefore, the reforms represented an official and decisive break with Nehruvian socialism and transformed India's teleology—as publicly perceived—in one decisive blow. In other words, the nation was no longer going where it had been going since 1947. Needless to add, this changed Indian cinema entirely, although it was only in 1994 that Sooraj Barjatya's *Hum Aapke Hain Koun..!* (*HAHK*, 1994), the key film to reflect this changed perception of the nation, appeared.

The sense that things had changed forever in India can be found in several films before *HAHK*. Parental figures (especially mothers) had often embodied tradition and had, therefore, been the conduit through with ethical values passed into the story, but this transforms in the early 1990s. In *Damini*, for instance, the heroine's parents are brazen opportunists, and the male protagonist's parents, who abet in the concealment of the rape, are duly jailed. This will be dealt with separately in the book, but parental figures represented a surrogate past of some kind and India was now in the process of repudiating its political past. Another significant film from the period Abbas–Mustan's *Baazigar* (1993) can be described as about two families fighting for the control of an industrial empire. Evidently, it portrays this not in terms of hostile takeovers and boardroom battles, but as a revenge drama with the male heads of the families hacking away at each other at the climax! But the most interesting part is that at the bloody culmination, the police watch from a distance without stepping in as though it would be inappropriate for the liberal state to intervene in a clash between business rivals, as it had been doing through state-run financial institutions in the socialist era.

Sooraj Barjatya's *HAHK*, a film generally taken to represent the commencement of the new economic era in popular Hindi cinema, is illustrative of a breed of films that took hold of the popular imagination in the 1990s, films with titles running to a full sentence, usually abridged in everyday parlance to acronyms. The film was enormously successful and was marketed as 'clean' entertainment because it avoided violence and sex, sticking determinedly to romance. *HAHK* is elemental in its simplicity and tells the story of marital ties between two families, those of an industrialist (Alok Nath) and a scholar (Anupam Kher) who were former college mates. The film moves from celebration to celebration connected with matrimony, and this means that enormous amounts of food and confectionary are incessantly consumed. There is virtually no world outside the family, but various social segments like the minorities (through a Muslim couple) and the lower classes (in the shape of servants) are given representation at the family gatherings—complete with songs and dances. The family gatherings in *HAHK* can be interpreted as the nation allegorized as a happy family—'Ramrajya', a political ideal (the rule of Ram) then invoked by the Hindu right wing. An even bigger hit than *HAHK* was Aditya Chopra's 1996 film *Dilwale Dulhania Le Jayenge (DDLJ)*, set in London and about non-resident Indians imagining an ideal community in India. Shah Rukh Khan, who made his debut in *Baazigar* as an anti-hero, played the male lead here opposite Kajol as a seemingly amoral person with no ties in India who reveals that he respects tradition deeply. There was arguably some apprehension in Indian minds about the moral fabric of society with

34

the demise of Nehruvian socialism, and Shah Rukh Khan's *DDLJ* persona draws upon the moment when the political ethic propounded by it had just vacated the national space, and heroes needed to draw directly from tradition to remain moral beings.

A fundamental aspect of the new cinema results from the perceived withdrawal of the state from the national space—hinted at in *Baazigar*—which means that there are several films in which the nation is allegorized as an ideal community constituted by rich/privileged people. In Aditya Chopra's *Mohabbatein* (2000) it is an exclusive school; in Sanjay Leela Bhansali's *Hum Dil De Chuke Sanam* (1999) it is the household of a musician-guru in which the high culture of the nation flourishes. This privileging of the nation without the mediation of the (withdrawing) state finds another kind of expression in Mani Ratnam's *Bombay* (1995), perhaps the only film hitherto to feature a Hindu–Muslim romance, made possible by the nation becoming the transcendental object of loyalty. At the climax, when the police are unable to stop the riots in Bombay, the protagonist's gesture summoning the nation touches an answering chord in the mob. Also, instead of summoning 'tradition' positively as *HAHK*, past inter-religious enmity is blamed for the nation's ills and both tradition-minded fathers are killed—almost with relief. The protagonists' movement from their bigoted village to cosmopolitan Bombay broadly follows the deemed rebirth of the nation. The title of the film, I propose, does not only refer to the location of the action but also invokes the emblem of economically resurgent India in the 1990s, with the booming stock market. The Bombay blasts of 1993, it may be recollected, targeted the stock exchange because it represented a resurgent India.

Another category of importance in the 1990s is patriotic cinema, with examples like Vidhu Vinod Chopra's *1942: A Love Story* (1995) and J.P. Dutta's *Border* (1998). The Kargil War happened much later, and the cause for militant patriotism cannot be traced to any such sentiment in the public space. My own explanation is that the end of Nehruvian socialism eliminated conflict between classes in cinema, which informs films like *Damini*, in which a maid is raped by her employer. Some films like *HAHK* eliminate inter-group conflict altogether, but films can also use another solution to deny inter-group conflict within India, which is to push conflict to the borders of the nation. When the adversary is demarcated by space, it is

Pakistan; when it is separated by time, it is the British. Patriotism is still in evidence, but in decline by 2001 in Ashutosh Gowarikar's *Lagaan* (2001), in which the anti-British rhetoric is muted and even affectionate.

The term 'postmodern' may be forbidding to the lay reader but it refers to a phenomenon in the late twentieth century exhibited by texts that moved from the high seriousness of modernism to a kind of playfulness attributed largely to the conclusion of grand narratives (around the Marxist idea of historical progress, for instance) that had gradually lost their pertinence. A key feature of postmodern texts is their tendency to mimic other texts but blankly, as it were. The teleological shift for the nation as perceived by Hindi cinema can be understood in this context as the conclusion of a grand narrative (of Nehruvian socialism), and it, therefore, engenders symptoms that might have been considered 'postmodern'. I refer here to the 'pastiche', especially in films starring Govinda, films like David Dhawan's *Hero No. 1* (1997) and *Jodi No. 1* (2001), in which films of an earlier period were consciously mimicked but blankly, without their becoming a parody. Govinda as an idol has a comic appeal different from others like Shammi Kapoor, who also did comic turns in lead roles. Where Shammi Kapoor's characters corresponded to social types or archetypes (for example, a spoilt young businessman in *Junglee*, 1961), the heroes played by Govinda do not embody types or archetypes drawn from social experience as much as the archetypal film hero as pastiche, and his films benefit by references to popular films. *Hero No. 1* makes a conscious reference to *Bawarchi*, without displaying that film's seriousness, while *Jodi No. 1* has protagonists called Jai and Veeru after the characters in *Sholay*. Another film which can be understood as postmodern pastiche is Ram Gopal Verma's *Rangeela* (1996), which is set in the film world. The movie *1942: A Love Story*, while being patriotic, also has many of the characteristics of the nostalgia film, which Frederic Jameson identifies as pastiche and places in opposition to the historical film. The nostalgia film mimics a 'look' without the enquiring intent of the historical film.

An account of the 1990s will be incomplete without attention to a new kind of thriller/gangster film exemplified by Ram Gopal Verma's *Satya* (1998), which differed from the earlier kind represented by *Agneepath* in being visceral in its realism. Its aesthetic anticipates that of later films like those of Vishal

Bhardwaj's *Kaminey* (2009) and Anurag Kashyap's *Gangs of Wasseypur* (2012), but it was one of a kind when it appeared. What *Satya* represents thematically can, however, be accounted for, because it shows the police not weak (as in *Agneepath*), but unfettered by the law. While this, interestingly, makes them highly effective, they are also no different from the various gangs, that is, they operate like private agencies rather than instruments of the state. Another related film providing insights into the attitudes of the 1990s is E. Nivas's *Shool* (2000), also co-scripted by Ram Gopal Verma. This film is about politics in the state of Bihar and about an upright police official (Manoj Bajpai) whose efforts in a town are subverted actively by a local politician named Bachchu Yadav (Sayaji Shinde). The film's conclusion shows the protagonist going to the state assembly when in session, evading the guards, striding up to Bachchu Yadav, and holding him down with a pistol to his head. After apologizing to everyone for the extreme step he is taking, he kills Bachchu Yadav. He then puts his gun down and salutes the nation ('*Jai Hind*') while the onlookers stand up in respect. The sight of a police officer invoking the nation and being patriotic is strange in popular cinema because its conventions once supposed that a police officer was not a mere employee of the state but actually embodied it within the narrative. If we see evidence of the state withdrawing from the public space in earlier films of the 1990s, what we notice in *Satya* and *Shool* means that the state is withdrawing from its own institutions as well. It is perhaps for this reason that the protagonist must invoke the moral authority no longer vested in his person but only in the abstraction of the nation.

The transformation of Hindi cinema in the 1990s consequent to the economic liberalization is the prelude to a more drastic one in the new millennium brought on by the advent of globalization. In the initial period, the global has some of the characteristics of the modern of the 1950s, and is as threatening, but with attractions as well. Since the prospects of modernity were uncertain, Hindi cinema had noir thrillers in the 1950s—like *Baazi* and *Howrah Bridge*—in which character ambiguity owing to modernity is responsible for the 'darkness', and an illustration is the heroine's father being a shadowy criminal and owner of a nightclub in *Baazi*. There is similarly a series of noir thrillers after 2000, perhaps beginning with Amit Saxena's *Jism* (2003), which deal with an adulterous and murderous woman whose moral vocabulary has been acquired outside India or in an apparently globalized milieu. Where the early films of the series associate adultery with murder, Karan Johar's *Kabhi Alvida Na Kehna* (2006) associates it with love, and perhaps represents the moment when globalization ceased to be a threat to the moral fabric of Indian society.

The Mechanics of Allegory

An issue that will engage the reader will be the mechanism through which political situations are so sharply allegorized by Hindi cinema, such as the mother-as-bread-provider in *Anmol Ghadi* allegorizing the land, and the bald south Indian trying to manipulate the north-Indian woman in *Padosan* corresponding to the leaders of the Syndicate (notably Kamaraj) attempting to control Mrs Indira Gandhi between the time she became prime minister and till she broke away by splitting the Congress. When would such allegorizations emerge and will there not be a lapse in time before this happens? This is a tricky question, but there has been some research that provides us with a clue. Apart from Jameson's formulation that all Third-World texts can be read as national allegories, a study by Beatrix Pfleiderer of audience reactions to popular Hindi cinema testing several independent hypotheses on its social role concluded that it was largely an instrument of 'cultural continuity'. Hindi films apparently stabilize the social system by representing new needs and mythologizing tradition. New needs are historically created and an instrument of 'cultural continuity' may need to bridge the gap between expectations aroused by tradition and the actual dispensations of history. What popular cinema apparently does is to problematize the experience of history in a language familiar from tradition and then provide reassuring fictional resolutions. This implies, as one might argue, that the expectations of the immediate present are the key to what is problematized and not past events. *Anmol Ghadi*, as already indicated, allegorizes the *expectations* from the Partition, which was expected a year later, and *Padosan*, which feels alarm at south-Indian machinations, provides a fictional resolution reassuring to north Indians. The drastic changes in Hindi cinema brought about by Independence did not arise from it as much as the expectations from it, such as the likelihood of the modern eroding traditional values and the state machinery functioning as a moral agency. Similarly, the Sino-Indian War did not lead to an allegorization of military defeat but to other representations, chiefly notions associated with the independent nation losing its sanctity. What the films after 1962 reflect or represent is weakening of nationalist sentiment and not regret of military defeat. Sometimes, as with the economic liberalization of 1991, the expectations take time to emerge, which is why *HAHK*, generally understood as the first film of the liberalized era, came out only in 1994, nearly three years after the momentous event. This film, again, does not allegorize economic liberalization as much as anticipate public attitudes towards the end of Nehruvian socialism.

2

The Grammar and Aesthetics
of Popular Hindi Cinema

In the Introduction, I noted how popular Hindi cinema rejected mimesis in the Aristotelian sense, holding certain truths to be greater than empirical reality, and that popular cinema was really intent upon the communication of these truths. If to D.G. Phalke, the Puranas and the epics were a perennial source of these truths, later-day socials continued to enact stories in the same heroic way, although they were ostensibly set in the contemporary world. Popular cinema had no place for ordinary beings even when the protagonists were poor, and this is why characters like peasants or farmers in *Mother India* or *Upkaar* are conceived of as heroic or mythical rather than ordinary people. This chapter is about the grammar of popular Hindi cinema, and it will try to show how these philosophical preoccupations on the purpose of arts and literature led popular cinema to a unique grammar and aesthetic in India that sets it apart and has helped it dominate its own turf in commercial terms, when better-established cinemas succumbed to global Hollywood. Since popular Hindi cinema's professed intent sets it apart from Aristotelian mimesis, it would be helpful to compare it with the neo-Aristotelian principles of classical storytelling from Hollywood, exhaustively studied and categorized by scholars like David Bordwell. This effort should, however, be accompanied by a word of caution: Hindi cinema has not attempted to theorize about its aesthetics and its grammar, and whatever is said here is deduced through observation of practice which has undergone changes, but not so much as to make the underlying perceptions unrecognizable. The precepts of the other arts in India have also been taken into consideration while speculating on the narrative methods of popular cinema.

A narrative film, David Bordwell notes, consists normally of three systems, the representation of space (mainly composition and orientation), the representation of time (order, duration, repetition), and

narrative logic (definition of events, causal relationships, and parallelisms between events). Scrutinizing
popular Indian cinema under the three systems will
be helpful to us, and we may, therefore, commence our
enquiry by doing so, then going on to examine other
aspects that they may lead to.

The Representation of Space

The mimetic urge makes it necessary for cinema to
preserve the verisimilitude of space through various
devices. A scene is a series of shots collected together
usually in a single locale or adjacent locales and
durational continuity is assumed. There are two ways
in which space is established, either immediately or
gradually. The 180-degree ('axis of action') system
ensures that shots are filmed and cut so that the spectator is always on the same side of the story. If an onward
journey is shown through an automobile moving from
left to right, then right to left signifies the return journey. Shot and reverse shot editing helps make narration
covert by creating the sense that no important sceno-
graphic space remains unaccounted for. The effects
of the cut and the close-up then become exclusively

dramatic or psychological and only provide emphasis. Within the scene, eyeline match uses character glance as a clue to link shots. The earline match also helps to convey the axis of the action. If a character cocks his ear to the right and we hear footsteps on the soundtrack, the person entering must move to the left. The way in which a character exits from one scene and makes an entry into another one (by including the time element) tells us the relationship between the spaces in the two scenes. Off-screen space, therefore, functions as a blank area, a 'screen' that invites the spectator to project hypothetical elements on to it and the entire space of the narrative is, therefore, created in the spectator's mind as one continuous whole.

The eyeline match, earline match, and the axis of action are as useful to Hindi cinema as to Hollywood since they eliminate the possibility of confusion within a scene, but the narrative space is not unified. Instead of gradually defining the totality of the space through the cut or the tracking shot, Hindi films tend to use the medium shot to catch the action within each designated space. The totality of each space is not established, but its quality is suggested. Films, in effect, denote the space of the action in each scene as an abstraction (such as 'courtroom', 'office', 'affluent household', 'police station', or 'hospital'), although it is generally acknowledged that, being an imprint of physical reality, the photographic/cinematic image cannot represent abstractions in the manner of verbal language. Cinema has no means to communicate the notion 'house', because any cinematic image will be a specific one: of a particular house filmed at a definite moment (a hillside cabin seen in the afternoon). But in popular Hindi films, there is an effort to define narrative space not as singular and continuous but as a collection of discrete settings, conceived as abstractions with each space denoted separately by its inherent qualities. An early film much cited by film theorists for a variety of reasons is Mehboob Khan's *Andaz*, and the way it represents houses in terms of their qualities is revealing. Both protagonists Raj and Neena (played by Raj Kapoor and Nargis) are enormously wealthy and both have huge houses in Bombay; Neena has one in the hills as well. While Neena's hillside home is associated with her years of maidenhood (in the company of her father), her city home is her residence as wife and mother. Neena does not return to her hillside home after her father's death (and her subsequent marriage) and it is as though the two spaces correspond to two exclusive conditions. Secondly, a house in the hills differs from a city one in occupying one floor while an affluent city home is two-storeyed and has a winding staircase, which is true of both Raj's house in Bombay and Neena's. Since both houses are alike, the film employs another strategy to differentiate between them. Neena has no mother while Raj's is still living. When we see Raj's house for the first time, therefore, his mother is standing conspicuously at the door, that is, his house is a 'house with a mother', which is different from Neena's, which is 'motherless'.

This denoting of each space in terms of its quality is easy to recognize when films are shot on sets but difficult in later films shot on real locations, and a handy example is J.P. Dutta's *Border* (1998), a war film shot in the Rajasthan desert. This film is about a war between India and Pakistan in 1965, but it is without an element that war films portraying strategy on the battlefield are rarely without maps. The presence of a map might have demarcated the space of the action into separate related areas, rendered the space less of an abstraction, but 'battlefield' is what is sought to be signified, and flat desert space is as close as one can get to the notion, since its demarcating features are limited. But regardless of later tendencies like location filming, popular cinema remains true to its original vision in declining either to establish the totality of each space or acknowledging off-screen space.

The Representation of Time

Universal time is a given in most cinemas, and in a scene's expository phase, narration specifies the time, place, and relevant characters. The time is assumed to be after the previous scene (unless otherwise suggested) and the previous scene indicates when this scene must occur, the device of the appointment or the deadline used by Hollywood is also used. (If someone makes an appointment for a week from today, then a week has lapsed in the narrative when the two meet next.) If there is no prior intimation of the time in any scene, an indication is given at the start of the scene (a calendar, a clock, or dialogue) to announce its place within the film's time scheme. When scenes are played out in different sets or locales, they represent different lines of action. Cross-cutting between different lines denotes simultaneous action. Within each line of action, the events are consecutive, but between lines of action taken as wholes, the temporal relations are simultaneous. This can be illustrated through this scenario: the hero gets up late in the morning; cut to the boss looking at the clock; hero eats breakfast; cut to the boss pacing up and down; etc. Denoted inevitably in each film is the duration of the action, the time taken for the entire narrative to unfold. Films also frequently furnish historical markers in order to contextualize a story, that is, 'fixing' the chronology of the narrative within a commonly accepted temporal framework, like 1939 to 1945 representing the course of the Second World War in a Hollywood war film.

In popular Hindi cinema, the sense that the action portrayed in each narrative is exemplary in some way (as they are in the epics and Puranas) implies that the context lacks significance. It can be argued that once the context loses significance, so does the historical moment since meaning then becomes eternal, in a way. Each film has a message associated with the trajectory of the protagonist(s); it is perhaps this sense of the eternal validity of its message that makes the popular film indifferent to universal time. The absence of off-screen space is a tacit denial of simultaneity, and this strategy points to the same thing. As regards duration, the notion becomes important because of the need to compare parallel action (such as, 'even before the appointed hour he found that his friends had arrived at the spot'). Since parallel action is denied, duration is also not in evidence. The international acceptance of *Lagaan* may owe largely to its having a definite duration—the three months' deadline given to the Indians to get their cricket team together and prepare for the match against the British. Other consequences of the denial of universal time include the flashback not having special significance as *action recollected*. Rearranging the past and present in chronological order does not impact a Hindi film containing a flashback. Devdas' childhood in the film versions of Sarat Chandra's novel, for instance, can either be placed at the beginning of the film or rendered in flashback. To describe the narrative construction aptly, one could say that episodes follow each other as tableaux. Since history presupposes universal time, we may now examine its treatment by Hindi cinema.

History and the Hindi Film

To begin, locating the action within a historical context confers distinct advantages upon any narrative. If the opening frame of a film says '1945', and the film itself is set in the United States of America, we recognize an allusion to the end of the war; we anticipate tumult, the music, and the returning soldiers. The allusion does not necessarily pertain to the past; it can be contemporary or even invoke the future (or rather, our expectation of it). The allusion is a sign that creates an instantaneous context. We become involved in the story on the basis of what we already know of the moment and we expect the drama in the film to be driven by its implications. The historical anchoring of the narrative is often compulsive and even futuristic fantasies specify dates. Most films set in the contemporary world also have an element of topicality that anchors them to the historical present.

The disinclination of popular Hindi cinema to attach itself to a historical context even when the discourse is political is illustrated by *Mother India*. As discussed previously, it is a remake of *Aurat*, also made by the same director, but *Mother India* sets its eyes on the optimistic nationalism of the Nehruvian era and is conceived as a 'national epic' replete with Soviet-style lyrical agrarianism. Although the film has a framing sequence suggesting a mechanized India of the 1950s, it makes no explicit references to the real political and historical events of its time. The events in the film are apparently spread over several decades but, apart from the customary greying of heads, it provides no credible markers to convey a real transition. The framing sequence shows the elder son grown up and dressed in the garb of a statesman, but the central narrative declines to contextualize itself in the freedom struggle, which might have justified his representation in this way. Where the drama in a Soviet film might have been played out against the backdrop of the revolution or the collectivization campaign (as in Eisenstein's *The General Line*, 1929), the drama in *Mother India* is innocent of events outside its own narrative.

The metanarrative of history (and universal time) presents each narrative with the opportunity of attaching itself to a common referential and provides the drama in the film with a universal context. Popular Hindi cinema does not acknowledge a universal context, and each narrative must, therefore, erect its own referentials. When Indian films deal with historical characters, whether in *Mughal-e-Azam* or Ashutosh Gowariker's *Jodhaa Akbar* (2008), they are love stories or family dramas in costume. Any kind of historical detail provided is subordinated to the motif of love; this is not true of a film like *Anne of the Thousand Days* (1969) or *A Man for All Seasons* (1966). Another kind of historical film (noted in chapter 1, 'The Historical Trajectory of the Hindi Film Narrative'), deals with India and the British or India and Pakistan and can be broadly termed patriotic rather than historical, some relevant examples being *1942: A Love Story* and *Border*. Here again, the specific political circumstances under which the events depicted occurred are irrelevant, and only the emotion of patriotism is key. A third kind of Hindi film now relevant is the 'political film', which has gained ground in the past decade. This category—represented by Rakeysh Omprakash Mehra's *Rang De Basanti* (2006) and Prakash Jha's *Raajneeti* (2010)—also relies on patriotism, though of a more civic kind. Where most patriotic films evoke feelings by demonizing an external enemy, these films demonize an internal one, but towards the same end. The mythic connections of the political film are admitted by *Raajneeti* when it draws explicitly on the Mahabharata.

A fourth category that needs to be acknowledged is the gritty, urban gangster film filmed in real locales, usually Bombay, like Ram Gopal Varma's *Satya* and Vishal Bhardwaj's *Kaminey*. The exceptional visceral quality of the action could lead one to regard these films as responding historically to today's politicized milieu, but this is illusory, although some political issues they invoke, like anti-north-Indian politicians in *Kaminey*, are recognizable. My own understanding is that their narratives create love- and hate-objects while following the trajectory of the protagonist(s) as in earlier films, but give the hate objects a political garb. Instead of the smugglers and dacoits from the 1970s' cinema we have political goons of the new millennium, but once this substitution is spotted, the central drama revolving around heroism and love becomes familiar. The politician in *Kaminey* is 'depoliticized' when he eagerly consents to abandon his anti-north-Indian stance for money. An actual politician would need to exhibit more loyalty to his constituency.

As films are shot increasingly on actual locations—of a particularly grimy sort—my tendered hypothesis about narrative time in Hindi cinema may become more difficult to sustain. But I would contend that *Kaminey*'s 'darkness' is no less mythical than *HAHK*'s family happiness. If a key marker were to be identified that transforms the real world invoked by the films into a mythical one, it would be their use of music. The background score in films like *Kaminey* is noisy, incessant, and dramatic, and there is an absence of silences where sounds from the actual milieu might have been heard. I see this as a way of suppressing—through aural means—the reality that the visuals emphasize, thus making its world mythical and placing it outside the flow of historical time.

The Family, Genealogy, and Romance

The employment of the family as a motif by Hollywood is often perceived as ideologically loaded, and the transformation of the family in films is also said to reflect the changing perceptions of the public. An aspect of family life that is consistently valorized is the issue of marital fidelity, as in *Arbitrage* (2012) in which a crooked fund manager needs also to be unfaithful to his wife to stand truly condemned. At the same time,

there are films in which the family plays no part—
like some all-male adventure films—and the family is
not an essential component of plot construction. The
family in Hindi cinema has also transformed, especially
in the last decade or so, but it is nonetheless differently
placed, if recent cinema is a reliable index. While the
family's presence appears more essential, it is not made
sacrosanct—as Hollywood treats the nuclear family—
suggesting that it plays another role in the narrative
than simply extolling tradition, as one might have once
concluded from domestic melodramas, especially films
like *HAHK*.

There are two sides to the representation of the
family in popular Hindi cinema, and if one is genealogy or the family's past, the other is romance, the
culmination of which leads to family formation. For
a long while, Hindi cinema could not do without
parental presence, and the easiest reading was that the
parental figure represented tradition. The parental figure, however, need not have been an actual father or
mother but could also be a surrogate. The Thakur in
Ramesh Sippy's *Sholay* (1975) is, for instance, a surrogate parent to Jai and Viru, the male protagonists.
This is not to say that all parents and their surrogates

are morally exemplary in their conduct, but there is a sense to be got that those straying from tradition (often by being Westernized) are also those who were not moral exemplars. Still, moral arbiters are provided, as in Raj Kapoor's *Bobby*, in which Raj's snobbish parents are contrasted with the free-spirited Jack Braganza, Bobby's father.

Genealogy is the family past, and making an appropriate comparison with Hollywood, the mythical genres from Hollywood like the western and the gangster film draw moral sustenance from America's past, the gangster film regretting the loss of what the western affirms. Even a revisionist western like Robert Altman's *McCabe & Mrs Miller* (1971) affirms a past dream (of enterprise) by dealing with its destruction because of the growth of monopolies. Since tradition in Hindi cinema—admittedly a nebulous term—may have had the same positive connotations that the pioneering past had for the western, one could suppose that the parental presence represented a surrogate past ideal of some kind for Hindi cinema, necessitated by its insecure ties with actual history. Since tradition is less eulogized now we need examine other functions that genealogy may be performing.

Looking once again at Hollywood's use of history, it is difficult to conceive of a narrative without a historical context to which it is anchored, at least the historical present. Even other-worldly fantasies need a historical context like 'the history of Middle-Earth' in *The Lord of the Rings* trilogy (2001–3). *Star Wars* (1977), if one recollects, begins with the legend 'A long time ago in a galaxy far, far away' implying a temporal context. Hindi films, since history cannot provide with contexts or 'locate' their narratives in universal time, may rely on the family past even when tradition is not eulogized. In *3 Idiots*, *Guru* (2007), and *Bunty Aur Babli* (2005), the parents, though not eulogized, are nonetheless present.

Tradition had connotations that were not only cultural or religious but also political, and were associated with the Nehruvian nation. When India moved out of the Nehruvian mode, there was a sense that it had moved away from tradition in some way and there are films like *Damini* and *Bombay* in which the parents are prejudiced and self-serving and rejected as moral arbiters. In *3 Idiots* and *Bunty Aur Babli* parents are seen as obstructions, while in others like *Dabangg* (2010) they have a strong presence but a small moral role. In each of these cases, the narrative is anchored in the parental figure as surrogate context. Sociologists may be tempted to attribute genealogy in films to the extended or joint family being important in the life of an Indian, but we would then expect it to be represented as sacred as well, which does not happen consistently.

If genealogy has the role of surrogate context, what is the role of romance? It is difficult to imagine a Hindi film in which there is no romance or love, and each film usually ends with love coming to fruition. An explanation that follows the last observation is that the culmination of a romance is a way of closing the narrative. The distinction between open and closed films is part of the debate on realism; in a closed film the world of the film is the only thing that exists, everything within it has its place in the plot of the film— every object, character, and action—in an open film, however, the world of the film is a momentary frame around an ongoing reality. Genre films are considered closed because the familiarity of their conventions and their repeating patterns exhaust the meaning of the narrative. A genre film exhibits the closure of a myth, and even a historical genre film can be described as imposing a final meaning upon the moment in a way that history itself does not.

Popular Indian films are closed films in a more basic way because their narratives are not located within the stream of history. Even a genre film like the western, because it locates itself within a historical continuum, can be said to leave itself open in some sense. The narrative ceases definitely at the conclusion of any popular Indian film, and this would not have happened if its links with the metanarrative of historical time had been authentic. As an illustration, Roland Emmerich's *The Patriot* (2000), an adventure film set during the time of the American Revolution, is a genre film with the Englishman Lord Cornwallis as one of its villains. This villain surrenders to the Revolution at the conclusion and the act brings the narrative to closure. Still, our awareness that the same Lord Cornwallis went on to become governor-general of India works, in some sense, against seeing the closure as final.

As already proposed, such historical links are foreign to popular Hindi cinema and, just as the family provides the narrative with a context, family relations must bring about the final closure. Where its links with history leave *The Patriot* opens to universal time, the autonomous, unhistorical universe of the popular film makes narrative closure necessary. The closure must be achieved at the level of the family (which is a social unit independent of history) and triumphant love is the readiest closure strategy. In the occasional film that has no place for romance, such as Bimal Roy's *Do Bigha Zamin* (1953), the coming together of the family still facilitates the final closure. In a film dealing with actual history, such as Chetan Anand's *Haqeeqat* (1964), set in the Sino-Indian War of 1962, the film concludes with the protagonists dying together facing the enemy holding hands.

If one considers the way film narratives are generally constructed, a strategy used in the closure is for the protagonist(s) to enter a new state—a realization must dawn on them (even if it is in death), they must have learnt something, overcome obstacles, or understood that an obstacle is insurmountable; or a success or failure must be admitted or recognized—and it is convenient for this change to be aligned with the natural states in a person's life, generally accepted as infancy, childhood, adulthood, and old age. The recognition at the closure of any film hence corresponds to the transitions between states: the maturing of an individual (childhood to adulthood) or his/her weakening and defeat (adulthood to decrepitude). In Hinduism, the states recognized are the ashramas—childhood, *brahmacharya* (the unmarried state), *grihasthashrama* (the householder), and *vanaprasthashrama* (retirement)—and the closure hence needs to be aligned with these states instead. Since the transition from brahmacharya to grihasthashrama is a crucial one when dealing with young people, marriage (the culmination of a romance) becomes the key event in the closure. It may be noted that in a Western 'romance' like Jane Austen's *Pride and Prejudice*, the protagonists move from immaturity to maturity rather than from the unmarried to the married state.

Motivation and Causality

There are many kinds of causality that can operate in a narrative, and one of the simplest is individual motivation or psychological causation, which is preferred by Hollywood. The classical formula for the Hollywood film involves psychologically defined individuals who struggle to solve a clear-cut problem or attain specific goals. In the course of the struggle, the characters enter into conflict with others or with external circumstances. The narrative ends with a decisive victory or a

defeat, a resolution of the problem and clear achievement, or non-achievement of the goals. The principal
causal agency is thus the character, a discriminated
individual endowed with a consistent set of evident
traits, qualities, and behaviours. In its early years,
Hollywood relied more on coincidences, which had
been the staple of melodrama and popular nineteenth-
century theatre. But with the growing emphasis on
realism around the turn of the century, coincidences
became less acceptable. Hollywood, of course, also
permits impersonal causes, but they are usually subordinated to psychological causation. Impersonal causes
may initiate or alter a line of story action, but personal
causes must then take over and move the narrative.
Coincidences and accidents must confine themselves
entirely to the initial condition. In the structure of the
classical Hollywood film, causes are also left dangling
to be picked up subsequently by effects. This method
leads the spectator to anticipation and guarantees that
the action does not slacken between any two scenes.
To illustrate the structure with a well-known film
Sam Raimi's *Spider-Man* (2002), Peter Parker becomes
super strong by accident, but his psychological condition induces him to take advantage of the accident, and

each episode is connected to the succeeding one in a similar way. Peter then needs a car to win Mary Jane but he does not have the money. He eventually finds a possible source but still needs to wrestle to get it. He wins the bout because of his 'spider-strength', but the manager cheats him. Peter encounters the robber just after he has been cheated, but allows him to escape because of his anger at the manager. The robber kills Peter's uncle because Peter permitted him to get away. Peter Parker resolves to fight crime because of his own part in his uncle's death. The causal connections are devised as a series of links in a chain and one cannot remove a link without affecting the plot adversely.

Popular Indian cinema differs in two crucial ways from Hollywood. In the first place it is not inclined to rely on psychological causation, because characters are ideals not endowed with psychology and, secondly, they rarely initiate action. The dastardly villain is rarely associated with a deliberate conspiracy and he is evil by nature, that is, without the quality being directed towards a purpose, as in *Sholay*. Consider, also, the clash that usually concludes an adventure film before the inevitable family reunion. Most of these fights take place after the figure of hate has been created and his treacherous nature elaborated upon. Yet, when the moment actually arrives for the villain to be dealt with, the final act of his disposal is postponed time and again on the most unconvincing grounds. If this method of storytelling prolongs the action, the reader will point out that most action films use the method to wring the greatest amount of excitement out of climactic sequences. A distinction must nevertheless be made between the villain's end at the hands of James Bond and the culminating action in Indian film melodrama. The typical James Bond adventure puts the protagonist initially at a disadvantage but when the obstacles are surmounted, the film makes the destruction of the villain deliberate—and sometimes even contemptuously simple. Action sequences in popular Indian cinema usually arrange a more fortuitous end for the hate figure.

Instead of offering the spectator the pleasure of watching the premeditated annihilation of the hate object, these sequences actually disregard the potential for such excitement: in the first encounter between Jai and Viru and Gabbar in *Sholay*, the two are employed to kill the villain but instead of their going out in search of the villain (like the bounty hunters go out in search of their quarry in *For a Few Dollars More*, 1965), the encounter takes place when Gabbar's men raid the village. This is unassertiveness on the part of popular cinema, but the chosen shot construction and the linking work consistently towards it. If I were to illustrate the methods of the popular film through a hypothetical scenario, I would say that, rather than participate in the excitement of a mountain ascent, a Hindi popular film would, more probably, show the summit ascended: the active pursuit of an end is less sought than the end simply attained. It may be noted that in the Hindu epics, the initial 'disturbance' is caused when an evil thought is planted by a minor figure in a key player's mind, for example, Manthara in Kaikeyi's mind in the Ramayana, and Shakuni in Duryodhana's in the Mahabharata. If we are to understand the structure of the popular film narrative as a 'grammar', we can justifiably say that its construction is the visual equivalent of the passive voice. It chooses not to generate excitement through a consistent use of the active voice, as Hollywood prefers to. It can be proposed that the grammatical employment of the active and passive voice have some correspondence with free will and determinism.

As in the Hollywood film, there is an initial disturbance that gets the narrative moving, but the difference is that this initial disturbance loses importance in a Hollywood film once the narrative gets going. In the classic Hindi film story, the initial disturbance moves every subsequent event in the narrative, which are themselves not causally linked. The initial disturbance is often in the prehistory of the narrative and shown in a preamble as in Yash Chopra's *Deewar*. In this film, the 'angry' protagonist owes his emotional state to a humiliation in childhood and this defining event (the 'first cause') dictates his conduct ever after. Sometimes the first cause is not even within the film but referred to in conversation, and *HAHK* is an instance of this. In this film, Kailashnath and Siddharth Choudhury were college friends who loved the same woman. She married Siddharth Choudhury when Kailashnath gallantly stepped aside and chose not to marry. The friendship between the two men is sacred because of this 'sacrifice' and the film is about the two families being kept together by marriage alliances. The strategy of the first cause is not as conspicuous in recent cinema but continues less obviously. In *3 Idiots*, the gardener's genius son being sent to college with the identity of his employer's son is the (off-screen) first cause that activates the story, though one discovers it much later. The first cause, it can be proposed, resembles the events in one's past existence, which are deemed to affect one's fortunes more than those in the present life. It also has a parallel in the 'seed' or the 'germ' which in Sanskrit drama the action in a play emerges from.

Character Types

Intentional action deriving from the initial disturbance accompanied by strict causality between events allows the characters of the protagonists to develop in Hollywood films, which also contain character types that do not develop. In *Spider-Man*, for instance, the protagonists develop but Peter Parker's aunt and uncle remain frozen as types. It can be argued that development of character would be difficult without causal linking between events, and without intentional action being a guiding principle. In the introduction I had indicated that because popular films are derived from the epics and the Puranas, action takes place at the heroic level, and this means that films need to be instructive and convey a transcendental message which is 'truer' than empirical reality will permit. My proposition at this point is that for the message to be received clearly, characters need to be cast entirely as types. As an analogy, a fable will be ineffective if the characters are not defined in advance in terms of their essences— a fox needs to be cunning, a lion bold, and a monkey mischievous.

Detractors of popular Indian cinema will wonder if the tendencies described bear this kind of overt intellectualization; they will ask if the 'stereotypes' cannot be simply put down to 'inept characterization'. It must be remarked here that American films are also prone to using stereotypes, but that these stereotypes are differently conceived. To illustrate, a frequent stereotype is the housewife and/or mother becoming radicalized in her dealings with the male establishment, seen in *Norma Rae* (1979) and *Erin Brockovich* (2000) among others. Contrary to the model in popular Indian cinema, it is not the character that is stereotyped in Hollywood but the process. What is stereotypical is the way he or she develops and a familiar ploy is for a character, not a perfect specimen, to improve.

When films have narratives spread over prolonged (although indefinite) intervals, change must somehow be accommodated, but the popular film responds by asserting that the initial condition is inviolable. In films like Vijay Bhatt's *Baiju Bawra* (1952) and M.S. Anand's *Agneepath*, a child grows up to right an injustice done to his father. The child's attitude, arrested in implacability, is then carried forward entirely into adulthood to furnish the narrative with its raison d'être. When the boy grows up, the rest of the world has altered but little. The villain is not only sustained in an unsullied condition for the exclusive purpose of vengeance, but the hero must also cease to exist after his ends are achieved because his vengefulness defines him entirely. This is vastly different from the realism of Coppola's *The Godfather: Part II* (1974), in which the protagonist avenges himself impassively upon his father's murderer, now senile and beyond recollecting his victim from 20 years before. In *Agneepath*, vengefulness is the hero's innate condition and he may not depart from it. The hero does not, however, *actively pursue vengeance* because the passive mode of narrative does not permit this. It is more accurate to say that he remains in his condition of agitation until an alignment of circumstances eventually allows his vengeance.

This tendency to identify character with an 'essence' is consistently exhibited by popular cinema, although critics who valorize realism have sometimes treated it with derision. Film critic Chidananda Dasgupta notes that there is a pact between film-maker and audience, and that the popular film struggles to overcome the built-in naturalism of cinema, and to bend this medium developed in a Western technological society towards its own mythical style of discourse. A beard on Valmiki in the Ramayana, whether on film or on TV, he argues, is not a photographic record of a real beard on a real man, but the symbol of someone who is supposed, by tacit agreement between film-maker and audience, to be a sage. This is undoubtedly true, but it still may not be enough reason to reprimand it. The arts in India have tended towards the same kind of representation, and what is perhaps jarring is that this is in the cinematic medium rather than dance drama (in which there is a natural distance created by stylization). S.N. Dasgupta, an Indian art critic, writing on a Rembrandt etching *Christ before Pilate* remarked that Rembrandt, although a great artist, 'failed to put Jesus in proper perspective' because he dwelt on a passing moment. Indian artists would not have laid emphasis on any passing moment, but would have tried to discover the 'essence' of the object of creation. This suggests that high art in India has functioned by the same precepts as popular cinema.

Also pertinent here are the way songs are employed. Playback singers have been used to render songs, but few attempts made to 'match' the voice of the actual singer with that of the actor or actress singing it on screen. The method of rendering songs also prevents the association of individual singing styles with the character or personality of the actor. A disembodied singing voice is perhaps a guise like a hairpiece, like a pair of spectacles, or a beard, transforming a vital being into an abstraction, helping to reduce him or her to an immutable 'essence'. Neepa Majumdar notes the very small number of singing stars actually providing play-back. For almost five decades, every major film actress borrowed from the same singing voice, that of Lata Mangeshkar, and there are only a slightly larger num-ber of male playback singers. Where Lata Mangeshkar's voice lent itself to the norm of 'ideal femininity', the voice of her sister Asha Bhosle became associated with 'oozing sensuality'.

The character-type being an element in the message, it would be very inconvenient to infuse him or her with complexity, that is, make them embody more than one quality. Complexity in characterization would mean a character having seemingly conflicting but concordant traits. If Hindi cinema, given its proclivities, declines to make its characters complex, the same was true of Sanskrit theatre, which permitted a limited number of types for heroes and heroines. Hindi cinema has generally also associated qualities with professions, although the qualities may change when the profession is viewed differently in different periods. As instances, here are some professions represented in Hindi cinema with their associated qualities: doctor (selflessness), policeman (toughness), farmer (goodness, simplicity), businessman (affluence, generosity). To give some instances of impossible combinations, a seriously ill person cannot have negative moral qualities, and it is difficult to imagine a wicked man wearing spectacles, which are associated with scholarship. Genius cannot go along with industriousness if Rancho in *3 Idiots* is any indication. Romantic youth cannot be seriously employed since work would interfere with their capacity for romance. *Upkaar* has a heroine who is a doctor, but because her devotion to the nation draws her to the hero (a farmer), her profession/vocation does not conflict with her romantic appeal.

The Relay of Meaning

The sense that transcendental truths are relayed by the Hindi film has been a recurring one in the preceding discussions. M. Madhava Prasad, critic and academic, contrasts the 'relay of meaning' in popular Indian cinema with the 'production of meaning' in classical Hollywood cinema. The sense of the truth of the epics and Puranas being at a higher plane than empirical reality has an important consequence in that the world of each film is not inscrutable as realism or mimesis might insist, but has a transcendental meaning 'truer than the real', and the task of the film is to relay it. The 'production of meaning' also implies the presence of ambiguities that need to be interpreted, an exercise that Hindi cinema does *not demand*, since its meaning is on the surface. This meaning is often found seen in films such as *Kismet* (Fate), *Dhool Ka Phool* (Flower in the Dust), *Sangam* (Confluence), *Dil Ek Mandir* (The Heart Is a Shrine), *Sholay* (Flames), *Deewar* (Wall), and

Chirag Kahan Roshni Kahan (Where Is the Lamp and Where the Light?). Their relationship with the text is metaphoric rather than metonymic, suggesting that the film is an instrument for an abstract signification.

The Hindi film song—a constituent like no other in cinema outside India—also has characteristics that support this reading. Unlike in Egyptian cinema (to which Hindi cinema has been compared) songs are not vehicles for singing stars but are playback supported, an aspect that we have recently discussed. Moreover, the lyrics of the songs are not specific to narrative contexts; they make abstract significations about love, life, death, etc., which explains why they have lives of their own, an aspect hardly true of songs in Hollywood musicals. Songs in the Hindi film deserve a separate study, but one might propose that they are/were placed at key moments to reflect in a general way on the meaning of the action. In recent cinema, many songs are either in robust dance sequences, rendered in on-screen performances (like the 'dance number'), or are on the soundtrack without being 'sung' on screen. In either of these cases, the lyrics do not contribute to the narration, though they may echo sentiments broadly relevant or appropriate to the scene. The absence of causal linking between episodes makes each film episodic, and the insertion of a song here does not disrupt the action, as might have happened if the causal linking had been tight.

Since the message relayed by a film is universally valid (that is, non-contextual), it eliminates subjectivity from the narrative, and point-of-view is, therefore, absent. The camera eye is omniscient and this aspect can also be related to the traditional theatre having a *sutradhara* (controller of strings) or troupe manager who presents the performance. His task goes beyond merely 'reflecting' upon the action, since there is no event in the narrative that he has not ordained, and over which he has no control. The narrative and the performance are *his* domain and no action onstage can retain its mystery with him. The universe of the action, being entirely the creation of the sutradhara, cannot be 'unknowable' like in the real world, and it is a world with a purpose; unlike that of the Greek chorus, the role of the sutradhara is not interpretive.

It can be argued that point of view is essential to suspense and surprise since they rely on subjectivity, knowledge/information being withheld from some characters in the narrative. *Vertigo* (1958), for instance, relies enormously on Scottie's subjective viewpoint. Most Indian film critics acknowledge today that popular Indian cinema is indifferent to the attractions of suspense and surprise. There are many attributes that go with these elements, and one of them is to build up the spectator's sense of anticipation through tight, causal linking, with causes left dangling and subsequently taken up by effects. Introducing plot devices to conceal the outcome might be actually akin to obstructing the relay of meaning, and this cannot suit any film's purpose. There have been attempts at composing detective stories in popular Indian cinema, but these are hesitant. They rely on withholding one or two items of information from the spectator even as the camera eye remains omniscient. The emphasis placed by popular Indian cinema upon presenting the spectator with the familiar does not mean that every episode in the narrative only fulfils predictions. It will be more accurate to say that the emphasis is on 'how things will happen' rather than on 'what happens next'.

The relative paucity of silences in popular Indian cinema, which is noticeable, implies that much of what happens is expected. The films, therefore, do not attempt to shock or surprise us into responses as much as demand our complicity. The use of heavy music at emotional climaxes stresses the familiarity of the respective moments; they can perhaps be traced to a feature of its aesthetics that has been noticed: it is based not on cognition but on recognition, and the fan knows what to expect. It is a particular product of 'the aesthetics of identity', which has been contrasted by theorists to the 'aesthetics of opposition'. A typical product of the latter is the detective story, which functions, as a rule, on the basis of the reader's ignorance of the 'whodunit'.

Melodrama

The aspect of popular Indian cinema to have been studied most extensively by academics is perhaps its melodrama, and the familiar strategy is to regard it in the light of Western studies of the notion. Broadly speaking, melodrama is seen to indulge in strong emotionalism, moral polarization, and schematization; it portrays extreme situations and actions, overt villainy, the persecution of the good and the final reward of virtue, inflated or extravagant expression, abrupt changes in fortune, and dark plotting. Most of these attributes are also those of popular Indian cinema and this seems to justify using Western theories to understand it. Melodramas are seen to use strongly emotional material from everyday life—murder and crime, natural calamities, trials, arrests, and impoverishment. The dramatic violations of emotional relationships—mother losing child, spouses undergoing imprisonment, etc.—and the misfortunes inflicted upon characters that naturally draw sympathy, like defenceless girls and truthful men, are also favoured. Melodrama consoles, punishes, teaches, and rewards, and popular Indian cinema's degree of 'moral polarization' was only too apparent until the new millennium. But the impassioned speeches characteristic of films like *Awaara* or *Deewar* left the screen by the 1990s, and popular cinema became less vocal. Other characteristics—such as the introduction of the unexpected into the action for instance, Pooja's accidental death in *HAHK*—continued.

The origins of Western melodrama have been located by Peter Brooks within the context of the French Revolution and its aftermath when the traditional sacred and its representative institutions (church and monarch) lost their centrality. Instead of the traditional sacred, the Republic itself became the agent of morality, and melodramatic texts evolved to include a non-sacred 'moral occult', a metaphysical system that rewards virtue and punishes wrongdoing. Melodrama, as an aesthetic form is, therefore, regarded as corollary to the democratization of society and this gives it special value. The identification of Hollywood's domestic melodramas with women is a result of the 'feminization of mass culture' in the West, but this is not pertinent because Indian film melodrama addresses (in terms of gender) a more undifferentiated audience. It is also difficult to see any relationship between the French Revolution and Indian texts, since one cannot assert that stories from the Puranas like that of Raja Harishchandra are not melodrama. A key difficulty with linking popular Indian cinema's methods to Western models also arises out of similarities between Indian and Western texts having been noticed earlier outside cinema. Sanskrit drama is seen to resemble some of the work of Elizabethan playwrights. Common to both are plot contrivances like the writing of letters, the introduction of the play within the play, and the restoration of the dead to life. Similar devices in Shakespeare's *Romeo and Juliet* and Bhavabhuti's play *Malati-Madhava* are often cited, although the latter has a happy ending.

These affinities are shown as instances of how similar devices are often invented independently. Popular Indian cinema could, therefore, have arrived at some of its melodramatic methods independently of the West.

Regardless, there are key differences between Western melodramas and their Indian counterparts, seen in cinema as well. As an instance of a well-known novel with recognizably melodramatic characteristics as, Charles Dickens's *Great Expectations* many be considered. Apart from suspense and surprise—not to be found in Indian texts because they favour the omniscient eye—the novel arranges appropriate destines for each of its characters based on their failings and righteous acts, and teaches them lessons. This process of learning implies a degree of free will not readily found in the Indian texts. As a counter-instance, Raja Harishchandra does not learn lessons, because he is the essence of righteousness. If one were to contrast the two texts, where in *Great Expectations* Pip and Estella are taught humility, the story of Harishchandra instructs only the spectator or the listener through the exemplary subject.

Coming to cinema, among the most highly regarded of Hollywood melodramas are those of Douglas Sirk, such as *All That Heaven Allows* (1955). In this film as well, the protagonists come to a new level of understanding brought about by their trajectories, and this cannot be said of the characters in *Awaara, Deewar,* or *HAHK*, who remain unchanged in essence. Vijay in *Deewar* is nominally 'bad', but he does not regret his ways. Judge Raghunath in *Awaara* is subdued, not because he is contrite about his own excessive harshness, but because he has found out that the young man who confronted him in court is his son. Circumstances (already known to us) come to the judge's knowledge. Western and Hindi melodramas both incorporate a 'moral occult' in their narratives, but in the latter we are entirely privy to its workings—we see the gods deliberate upon Harishchandra's fate, and divinity also intervenes in *HAHK*, with the family dog as its agent.

Moral Instruction

In the previous chapter, I remarked that in Hindi cinema a Hindu name implies a 'person' and not someone specifically from the religion, and this implies a milieu in which religion confers identity only upon non-Hindus. But as if to allow for its mirror image, there is the genre of the Muslim social (often ventured into by Hindu film-makers) with films like *Mere Mehboob* and *Nikaah* (1982), in which everyone has a Muslim name with an occasional Hindu name signifying the outsider. One might argue based on Hindi cinema that Hinduism is not a faith as much as a social practice associated with the milieu. This goes along with Hinduism not admitting proselytizing. In the category of the Muslim social, correspondingly, Islam is not a faith but a set of social practices. Where films like *Ben-Hur* (1959) use miracles to induce faith, the Hindi film's portrayal of faith can even verge on self-parody, as in *Amar Akbar Anthony*. It is because of this non-recognition of faith that later films like *3 Idiots* treat religious affiliation as a mere inconvenience.

There are some paradoxical aspects to Hindi cinema that need to be acknowledged at this juncture. While it has been argued that it is the familiar that narratives set out to give expression to, there is also a supposition that Hindi cinema may instruct through a message. A question that will engage the reader is how something familiar to the spectator can also become instructive. This is speculative, but religious or moral instruction can be associated with proselytizing, while, in India, moral law is associated with dharma, a contextual system of ethics based on one's birth and station. This hypothesis also finds itself explaining the importance of genealogy in film stories—an aspect already commented upon. Since dharma is contextual there is none 'outside the pale' who needs instruction, as a proselyte would. It may, therefore, be proposed that the message is only a familiar assertion, although it takes the form of instruction. At the same time, their contextual natures make the tenets of dharma nebulous, and the messages can transform in new social circumstances. Where the message was once a moral one implicating loyalty to appropriate objects like parents, nation, community, family—a message gaining currency in the new millennium is that of self-fulfilment and the achievement of personal goals, with examples being *3 Idiots*, *Guru*, and *Bunty Aur Babli*. The greatest paradox is that while dharma is contextual, Hindi cinema presents the values it propagates as non-contextual. The contextual nature of dharma can be usefully applied to the categories of villains in Hindi cinema, which need to be explained.

Villains are those who cause harm to the protagonists, but harm need not necessarily come from a bad person and might be the result of a misunderstanding or failed communication, as in *Andaz*, or someone led astray by bad counsel (as Queen Kaikeyi was in the Ramayana). When one scrutinizes the actual bad people of Hindi cinema, one finds that until the 1960s, the villains were usually recognizable social types whose wrongdoings were typically associated with them not performing their given social roles fairly/correctly. Fathers could be wrongdoers by being authoritarian as in *Devdas*, *Taqdeer*, *Kismet*, and/or harsh as in *Awaara*. Mothers were usually emblems of correctness, but stepmothers and mothers-in-law could fail as role models. There are appropriate traits associated with someone deemed a wrongdoer, for instance, greed as exhibited by the moneylender/landlord who exploits peasants, as in Bimal Roy's *Do Bigha Zamin*, philandering as exhibited by the lover played by Premnath in Raj Kapoor's *Barsaat* (1949), and malice as shown by the Brahmin priest Salomalo in Damle and Fattelal's *Sant Tukaram*. But lurking alongside this *dharmic* category is also a more shadowy figure, that of the professional criminal in films like *Awaara* and *Baazi*, someone who lies outside the scope of dharma and is 'evil'; one can associate these 'practitioners of evil' in the 1950s with an experience lying beyond the code of dharma, that of modernity. The villain in *Baazi*, for instance, is the owner of a nightclub and gambling den, vices associated with the modern.

From the early 1960s onwards, as indicated in the previous chapter, the milieu had to deal with something much more difficult—disillusionment with the nation following the Sino-Indian War—and Hindi cinema moves into its 'escapist' phase. Where film stories in the 1950s implicate the nation deeply, those following the Sino-Indian War do not; stories are resolved anyhow and the professional criminal becomes handy as in films like *Waqt* and *Jewel Thief*. The increasingly extravagant villains of the 1960s and 1970s may be interpreted as a measure of cinema's unresponsiveness to the nation and national issues. Where a courtroom confrontation reunites the family in *Awaara*, the villain does it in *Waqt* and *Yaadon Ki Baraat*. The allegorical aspect of the courtroom scene has already been elaborated on, but the villain had no such significance. Also, as an instance of the villain's independence of social models (where before they traditionally corresponded to social types and were given socially defining names), the one in *Bobby* goes by the same name as the actor who plays him: Prem Chopra. This reveals the film's lack of faith in its own fiction and shows that the villain is in the narrative only to affect a resolution.

These extravagant villains continue until the early 1990s, but with Nehruvian socialism officially abandoned in 1991, Hindi cinema's allegorical task became easier. It no longer felt compelled to implicate the state and its policies in each narrative, since the state had tacitly admitted that its intervention in social life had itself been an error. The baroque villains of the 1960s, 1970s, and 1980s abandon Hindi cinema in the 1990s, although the notion of the villain is not outmoded, and there is a reversion to dharma as a way of defining the wrongdoer. ViruS in *3 Idiots* is a teacher who oversteps his authority while self-interest takes precedence for even the less benign ones from *Om Shanti Om* (*OSO*, 2007) and *Kaminey* over the roles they are meant to perform.

Genres and Their Aggregation

While Hindi films can be categorized according to their narrative content it would be difficult to divide them coherently into genres except for a handful like the mythological film and the domestic melodrama, which have not exhibited stable conventions. Drawing from Roland Barthes, genres may be broadly regarded as engaged in creating enduring mythologies from historical moments, in a sense giving their exigencies eternal justification. The western, for instance, recalls the historical origins of the American nation. As argued earlier, Hindi cinema's temporal sense prevented it from responding to history and universal time, and this may also stand in the way of stable genres being formed around key events like the struggle for freedom, but there is also the issue of generically incompatible elements within a single film.

As already proposed, the popular Hindi film narrative is not structured as a chain of causes and effects, but are noticeably episodic, and arranged somewhat like a series of tableaux. It is this aspect of popular Indian cinema that is apparently responsible for its omnibus characteristic, that is, its comprising different, often unconnected items, the absence of generic differentiation, the presence of innumerable subplots, and other narrative digressions. This tendency, or rather the resulting heterogeneous genre, which I am simply calling an 'aggregation', has been variously described as a 'cinema of attractions', a 'bricolage', a 'conglomeration', and a 'cinema of interruptions'. As suggested by the terminology, each description of the phenomenon entails a different explanation about its purpose. Popular Indian films include diverse narrative elements that often lie outside the ambit of the domestic melodrama, but generic distinction remains an enormously difficult task for critics. Most examples include generic elements that find correspondence in Hollywood—the western, the gangster film, the heist film, and the horror film—and these generic elements can sometimes dominate the narrative. *Sholay* incorporates elements taken from the western; *Deewar* employs several motifs of the gangster film; and the Ramsay brothers have been renowned for their horror films like *Purana Mandir* (1984), but all of them include elements that belong in other genres (like slapstick comedy in *Sholay*). As in American genre films, the dominant elements in many of these films sometimes also determine the spectator profile. If 'youth films' like *Dil Chahta Hai* (2001) are meant for young audiences in the metropolitan cities, horror films that incorporate elements of magic are usually targeted at the small towns of northern India and may be classified as premodern in discourse. There was once a subgenre in which the actors were 'B' category stars, like Dara Singh and Sheik Mukhtar, and these small films were watched by a 'subproletariat' that was predominantly Muslim. The triumphs of big films like *Sholay* and *Dharam Veer* (1977) were due partly to their integrating motifs from these films with those of the domestic melodrama. The integration of (by Hollywood standards) incompatible elements into a portmanteau genre is only rendered possible because of the episodic structure of each film. The same episodic structure also admits other attractions like autonomous comedy sequences, songs and dances—increasingly demarcated as voyeuristic spaces within any film—and even religious interludes. It is also increasingly noticed that 'attractions' are not clearly demarcated from the narrative and, if one were to define it from today's films, one could say that an 'attraction' is simply a sequence that does not fit into the narrative logic and exists independently within the film. To illustrate with an example, in *Kaante* (2002), which has a narrative that splices Quentin Tarantino's *Reservoir Dogs* (1992) and Bryan Singer's *The Usual Suspects* (1995), two of the protagonists tip a Pakistani arms dealer over a balustrade and watch him plunging 20 or 30 storeys downwards. The episode serves no narrative purpose within the film and we are forced to read it as an autonomous attraction. Watching a Pakistani arms dealer plummeting from a high-rise is something a 'patriotic' Indian spectator might desire to see. It is the episodic structure facilitating the insertion of attractions and the narrative aggregation that also allows the incorporation of 'contemporary' elements into the story like the one just discussed. Interestingly, one of the definitions of the art of theatre to be found in the *Natyasastra* is that the art of theatre is no more or no less than the nature of the world with its happiness and despair presented through acting. This has been interpreted as meaning that Sanskrit drama is itself 'an aggregate of model situations'.

Devotion

One of the consequences of a contextual system of ethics is the absence of universal guiding principles on how people should act. Action is considered 'good' to the extent it is committed to reinforce the interconnectedness of empirical phenomena and ethical conflict is the tension between 'solidarity and separateness'. Still, a universal signifier is required to denote goodness in such a way that it addresses an undifferentiated mass audience. Devoutness is the accepted way of denoting this, perhaps because in absence of a universal social ethic the decision on righteousness rests with the gods. Devotion is essentially a narrative strategy: in some Hindi horror films vampires are equally vulnerable to the Cross, the Koran, and the Bhagavad Gita. Genuine devotion, it can be argued, is specific about the objects towards which it may be directed.

There is another interesting aspect to devotion in popular cinema that needs exploration. The idols worshipped in Hindu temples are conceived as objects of devotion and, while the Hindu gods are anthropomorphic, these idols are often mere cult symbols that do not imitate human proportions with any particular faithfulness. While the contention that idols are 'symbolic' will be contested, what is pertinent here is only that actual idols do not imitate human proportions faithfully. Theorists have invoked the tradition of darshana in Hindu worship where muteness on the part of the devotee and mediation by a priest are a prerequisite, but devout moments in Hindi films *do not follow this prescription*. The devoutness in popular cinema is usually directed towards idols that are sculpted in a (naturalistic, Western) way that makes their human attributes manifest. These gods are sometimes muscular and seem capable of movement, where traditional idols are solid in their immobility. Where the object of worship in a usual Shiva temple is a sculpted lingam (a stone phallus) a Shiva temple in a popular film enshrines a 'lifelike' statue of the god. This does not mean that we do not see *lingams* in popular cinema. As an instance, the pre-title sequence in *Satyam Shivam Sundaram* (1978) shows people worshipping a wayside stone shaped like a lingam to demonstrate that it is faith that renders the object of worship sacred. Yet, application to the divine in *Satyam Shivam Sundaram* is always made to anthropomorphic deities (usually Krishna and Radha) and devotion is also directed towards them in the song sequences. In many other films, the scenes are shot and edited during the devotee's address as though an actual dialogue was in progress. The entreating face of the character is cut to the reassuring countenance of the idol (often employing the eye line match and shot reverse shot editing) and the general sense is there is a communion between the two. What is intended is not to introduce a god to 'control psychic dispositions', but one is actually more mindful of material claims. What is presented is not only an icon more reassuring to the spectator but an accessible deity capable of intervening with human understanding in human stories. To conclude, the abrupt 'divine interventions' witnessed in popular cinema are extraneous to narrative logic and would not be accommodated within the narrative if the individual episodes were held together by causal linking. When Hollywood admits divine intervention (*The Ten Commandments*, 1956) god is implicated causality.

While commenting upon melodrama earlier, I observed that the genre allowed for abrupt changes in fortune, and it would seem that divine intervention is a way in which such changes in fortune can be effected. With the decline in the melodramatic content of Hindi cinema in the new millennium and the replacement of moral issues by self-fulfilment, the use of divine intervention in Hindi cinema as a device to effect changes has been on the decline, although the practice of religion has itself become a key issue in social life.

3

The Production and Distribution of Hindi Films

A Macro Perspective

The term 'Bollywood' used for popular Hindi cinema suggests that Hindi cinema had been institutionalized like Hollywood in the organization of film-making and distribution, but this is hardly a fact. Historically, the term 'studio system' applied to Hollywood refers to the practice of large motion picture studios between the 1920s and the 1960s of producing movies primarily on their own film-making lots using creative personnel usually under long-term contract, and dominating exhibition through vertical integration, that is, the ownership or effective control of distribution and exhibition. During Hollywood's Golden Age, the late 1920s to the late 1940s, eight companies constituted the so-called major studios with five among these eight being fully integrated conglomerates, combining ownership of a production studio, distribution division, and a substantial theatre chain, and contracting with performers and film-making personnel. Bollywood is not organized in this way and if one were to characterize it acutely one could say that it is highly decentralized and that films are financed informally through entrepreneurial capital. Contractual agreements are oral rather than entered into in writing, which implies that networks created by kinship and 'trust' are the conduits through which finance flows. This also means that legal recourse when contracts are not fulfilled is difficult and illegality, therefore, creeps into deals.

Unlike in Hollywood, there is little integration between film production, distribution, and exhibition, and all three areas are dominated by family-run firms with children usually following in their fathers' footsteps and inheriting businesses. The term 'studio' also has a different connotation here in that it is only the shooting space and does not include the aspects that a major Hollywood studio naturally would. Since a businessperson's success in the film industry depends greatly on his/her place in networks, people in one line often venture into other lines within the industry based on the influence they command: an actor could become a producer or a distributor of films. But this does not mean that outsiders cannot enter the industry, and it is generally known that a vast majority of film producers are outsiders who do not venture into more than one or two films.

The Indian film industry attracts a great deal of attention but in comparison with many other businesses in India, it is almost minuscule. At around $2 billion annually, the film industry is less than 2 per cent the size of the Indian real estate industry. India has been touted as the largest film industry in the world (based on the number of films made), but it is estimated that less than 10 per cent of the films made run profitably and a vast majority only lose money. Cinema has captured the imagination of the Indian public and film is an enormously glamorous business, but if the question of whether a reliable business model exists in the film industry arises, the answer would probably be a resounding no. Still, the influence of the film industry on other kinds of business cannot also be neglected, and it contributes in a big way to advertising and other kinds of entertainment like the music industry. It is perhaps because the intangibles associated with the film industry are so large that one cannot quantify its actual commercial impact reliably.

The Economics of Film Production

While most films fail commercially, those that succeed offer returns of a very high order—up to four times one's investment. But the risk is so high that banks and financial institutions do not finance film-making and private financing is needed with interest rates ranging from 36 to 48 per cent per annum. But with the high glamour quotient, money still keeps pouring into the film industry, from India and abroad from businesses as diverse as jewellery and diamonds, construction, and real estate; these tend to be managed informally and often through kinship ties. The active involvement of organized crime in the film industry and film-financing is also well known. Budgets for Hindi films range from Rs 15 million (about $250,000) to Rs 650 million (about $10 million) for the really glitzy features. Since films are sold on the basis of the stars appearing in them, the salaries of the stars can take up as much as

25 per cent of the total budget. In comparison, production and post-production costs take up only 35 per cent and 10 per cent, respectively.

As distribution is separate and decentralized, the country has been divided into five major territories going back to the pre-colonial era and which do not quite find correspondence with India's states as they are today. They are Bombay (part of Maharashtra and Gujarat), Delhi/Uttar Pradesh/East Punjab (including Jammu and Kashmir, Punjab, Delhi, and parts of UP), Central Province/Berar (Rajasthan, Madhya Pradesh, Chhattisgarh, and parts of Maharashtra), eastern (Bihar, Odisha, Bengal, and the North-East), and south (Andhra, Telangana, Karnataka, Tamil Nadu, Kerala, and parts of Maharashtra). With overseas receipts becoming important in the success of a film because of the higher admission prices, there is now also an overseas territory which is further subdivided into North America, United Kingdom, Gulf states, South Africa, etc. Distributors bid for territories for five to ten years as the valid period and further resell to others on the basis of a subdivision of territories; they, in turn, sell screening rights to exhibitors or receive advances. Distributors can either opt for outright purchase of a film for a specified period or distribution on a commission basis, where they hold back a portion of the receipts and remit the rest to the producer. A common arrangement is called the 'minimum guarantee', contracted before production commences, and is based on the stars, story, etc. Close to 30 to 40 per cent of the guaranteed amount is disbursed in stages during production while the rest is disbursed when the prints are delivered. This system places more risks on the distributor, but though it protects the producers, it does not guarantee that they receive the additional receipts they are entitled to if the film is hugely successful, because of a lack of transparency. Distributors tend to compensate for their losses on flops by holding on to receipts from hits. The fact that they are located far away from production centres also facilitates this. Apart from the five major territories, there are also 'A', 'B', and 'C' class centres, 'A' denoting the cities and towns where collection overflows (above the minimum guaranteed amount) are also easy. In B and C class centres, the producers have no means of ascertaining the receipts and rely on data from A centres as indicative of the success for the other two areas as well. Films were once released first in Bombay and later in the other cities, but, with the advent of video piracy, releases in major cities are simultaneous and alongside overseas centres like London, New York, and Toronto, that have sizeable markets for Indian films.

Within the exhibition hall, ticket prices were nominally fixed based on the distance from the screen, with the closest being the cheapest as well. In actual practice, the segregation was a way of differentiating between different social classes, with the working class seated right up in the front, the middle class in the middle, and the rear stalls and the balcony for the 'elite' (English-speaking) class. It is interesting that in the halls screening Hollywood films, the lowest class had far fewer seats, the assumption being that English speakers could not belong to the working class. The advent of the multiplex has seen such class divisions disappear, since admission into multiplex screens is more expensive than into single-screen theatres, and the class of clientele is naturally restricted. As a result, Hindi films have transformed in terms of their subjects in the new millennium because of their ability to target multiplex audiences in smaller halls. At the same time, there has also been a huge influx of migrants into the cities because of India's growth story and 'city audiences' are not what they once meant.

Putting a Successful Film Together

The most auspicious way for a film could start would be for a story idea to be related to a major male star by a writer, director, or producer who has not yet made a mark, and the star taking a fancy for it. Gradually, it would seem, the male star has become the most bankable element in a film. Many directors credit themselves with having created stars, but in the recent past, new stars—like Ranbir Kapoor—have often come from film families, and media publicity has preceded their film appearances. This means that the screenplay (or the writer) gets little importance, and there is no emphasis on the development of high-quality scripts. Film critic and academic Tejaswini Ganti has an interesting observation on how negotiation takes place: instead of proceeding through agents, there is a need for an actual face-to-face interaction between producer and star in which their respective hierarchical positions are established. For instance, a producer visiting the star at his home would be an indication of the star wielding more power. The writer in any film occupies a fairly low level in the hierarchy, with the choreographer and composer ranking above him/her. The 'side attractions' in any film—chiefly songs and dances—are often held to be more central to a film's success and those responsible for them also get due credit. There have nonetheless been writers who have become stars in their own right, and Salim–Javed rank as one of those whose dialogues resonate in people's minds even today. The dialogues from *Sholay*, *Deewar*, and *Mr India* are a case in point. But, by and large, song composers (and sometimes lyricists) have received greater importance.

The personal nature of the interactions places great emphasis on oral agreements as binding, and one senses a relationship between orality and hierarchical station. One could argue that while a written agreement makes relationships professional or impersonal, oral agreements become instruments of hierarchical power. It is perhaps for this reason that cast and crew are brought on board through narrated scripts—the director or the writer performing, as it were, instead of relying on a printed script. One detects in this strategy a continuation of the tradition in which a highly placed patron was the first recipient of a performance. Since the star is a key figure, the narration can be interpreted as an act of hierarchical submission by the director or writer, who has a smaller stature in the Indian film industry than the director-as-'auteur' has in Hollywood. This could also explain how top directors like Karan Johar and Aditya Chopra have gradually 'moved up' to become producers.

The 'mahurat' is a ritual associated with the commencement of film production and is fixed in consultation with astrologers. It can be a simple or an ostentatious affair, and one recollects full-page advertisements in the magazine *Screen* announcing films that were eventually shelved. The mahurat includes religious elements, but an enactment of a scene intended to represent the film is also filmed. This filmed sequence hardly ever finds a place in the final product. The mahurat serves as publicity and is often the basis on which finances are raised.

Songs and dances are an integral part of the final film and most of them survive in themselves as audio or video clips long after the film has faded from public memory. As already noted in the last chapter, songs strive for a level of abstraction that makes them stand alone as romantic poetry. Dances were once devices to portray inner feelings of some kind (such as yearnings and even dreads), but in the past decade or so there has been a greater incidence of 'fun' songs usually rendered at extravagant parties. With the emphasis on realism in recent cinema, songs have not disappeared but are heard on the soundtrack as the rest of the background score is. They are a key ingredient in the marketing of films, and the songs are released two months in advance to have them imprinted in public memory and also to make potential audiences curious about the sequences in which they appear. Outdoor songs are filmed in scenic locales often in Europe and in the mountains. One advantage of filming abroad is that the movements of stars can be controlled, and this is no mean advantage considering that many of them have the tendency of disappearing and disrespecting shooting schedules. This can have enormous consequences upon the cost of film-making, and shooting abroad actually becomes cheaper. Also, scenic Indian locations are being degraded quite rapidly while those in Europe have been zealously protected. It is, therefore, not unusual for a scene set in India to be filmed in Europe—say, Switzerland pretending to be Ooty in south India.

After 2000, satellite television has made some difference to film production by introducing an element of professionalism. Some production companies have also raised equity from the public through initial public offerings. Satellite television provides a way for films to recover part of their costs, but early screening of films on satellite television has also been found to adversely affect the collections, especially in B and C centres. Some television channels have also begun funding Hindi films, especially because they find it easier to leverage their activities by approaching banks and financial institutions.

Bollywood uses a specific terminology in its dealings, and the 'cost of the film' is understood to be the budget plus the promotional expenses. 'Gross collections' are the money realized through ticket sales while 'non-theatrical revenues' include satellite television rights, music rights, subsidies, etc. 'Net collections' are the gross collections less entertainment tax. 'Footfalls' pertains to the total number of tickets sold. The distributor share of the net collections in multiplexes decreases every week, with it being highest (50 per cent) in the first week, 32 and 37 per cent in weeks two and three, respectively, and 32 per cent thereafter.

In single-screen theatres it varies between 70 and 90 per cent on a steady basis.

The way in which the success of a film was decided and defined was the number of weeks a film ran. A 'silver jubilee hit' ran for 25 weeks, a 'golden jubilee hit' ran for 50 weeks, while the 'diamond jubilee hit' was a film which ran a full 75 weeks. Today, the emphasis is on recovering costs early, and even a second week is cause for cheer. One reason is that with the arrival of multiplexes there has been a sharp increase in the price of tickets (the average ticket price in a multiplex is Rs 140 and Rs 200 as against Rs 60 in a single-screen theatre), and the second is that there is much more competition with many more films being made. Then there is the incidence of piracy: films are available within days of a release, making audiences lose interest in it. In domestic screenings, for instance, where *HAHK* was released in only 500 theatres, *Ek Tha Tiger* (2014) was released simultaneously in 3,300 theatres. The result is that the benchmark is now Rs 100 crores in net collections (about $15 million), which an increasing number of films are able to achieve in the very first week. But with production costs also going up, this amount in net receipts is still inadequate for a film to break even, as in the case of *Ra.One* (2011), which had to rely on overseas collection and ancillary streams as well.

The Future for Hindi Popular Cinema as a Commercial Enterprise

A study conducted in 1991 declared that although India was the largest film producing country in the world, its earnings from foreign markets were not substantial, and the proportionate share had actually been higher in the 1970s. This is partly facilitated by overseas spectators paying substantially more for the price of a single ticket. To compare Hollywood and Bollywood, in 2012 Hollywood sold $1.36 billion tickets worldwide, while Bollywood sold $2.6 billion, but Hollywood grossed $10.8 billion compared to the Indian film industry's $1.6 billion; this means that the realizations per ticket by Hollywood were on average 13 times as large. The ratio of overseas to domestic earnings also differs, but for the big Hindi films, it ranges between a fifth and half. The overseas spectator profiles for Bollywood have changed significantly, and where Hindi films were watched widely in Africa and

Third-World countries, the overseas market has gradually become dependent on the Indian diaspora. One could say that Bollywood's strength on its own turf against Hollywood owes not so much to Bollywood's marketing capabilities as much as India being a cultural exception; this is lent strength by the fact that overseas audiences are largely from the diaspora.

There are two aspects that suggest that Bollywood is unlikely to spring surprises; its growth globally will be predictable. Firstly, it has not been inclined to explore new markets or create films especially for export markets; the size of the diaspora will, therefore, increase, but only gradually. Secondly, the Western countries where Bollywood has been realizing a bulk of its overseas earnings have moved away from the policy of cultural assimilation; migrants have retained their ethnic identities and formed groups that consume cultural products from 'home'. Another feature is that with the advent of globalization, a fair part of Bollywood's clientele in the cities is culturally closer to Indian migrants in the West than to their countrymen in the villages and small towns. It is not that these are greater in number but the per-ticket realizations in the city multiplexes makes them more important for big films. This split in the cultural identity of the Indian into the global kind and the 'desi' kind is a more unfathomable development than Bollywood's commercial achievements, and will be dealt with in the next chapter.

4

Global Bollywood

Hindi Cinema and Bollywood

The term 'Bollywood' used today to denote mainstream Hindi cinema from Bombay became widely accepted only in the new millennium, when Bollywood became a brand. The term was, as late as the new millennium, resisted by doyens of the film industry in India because they considered it to be pejorative, that is, indicating that mainstream Hindi cinema simply aped Hollywood. Among the two types of cultural nationalism at work with regard to the meaning of popular cinema today, the older one insists that mainstream Hindi cinema is first and foremost located at 'home', in India. The second sees a distinct cultural constituency including not only audiences within India but a cross-over segment as well and the term 'Bollywood', shorn of its pejorative implications, is promoted by 'cultural nationalists'. The indications are that the term 'Bollywood' first became acceptable not within India but in the USA as well as the UK, in places like Bradford, Leicester, and Birmingham, where Hindi films are marketed as a brand, with 'Bollywood' being a kind of label. Since a part of the overseas audience consuming mainstream Hindi cinema would be South Asian without being Indian, the term 'Bollywood' may have even become a more acceptable label than 'Indian', because it does not signify a specific national identity which might invite hostility. What makes Bollywood a brand is not the content of cinema—as constituted by film narrative—but an allure produced by a characteristic visual excess brought in by spectacle, choreography, costume, and music. It is this visual excess that allows Bollywood to become a 'lifestyle statement', and enables it to be employed in areas outside cinema itself. It is Bollywood and not mainstream Hindi cinema that has helped make Indian capital come to the forefront abroad through Indian restaurants/food, clothing, and decor. Well-known instances are the musical *Bombay Dreams* (2004) produced by Andrew Lloyd Webber and with music by A.R. Rahman, and the various marketing campaigns used partly by clothing stores and restaurants. The well-known British departmental store Selfridges had a month-long focus on the theme of Bollywood in May 2002 with Indian clothes and items of decor exhibited in its London and Manchester shops. During this period, a broad-based promotion of South-Asian film, dance, music, and theatre called 'Imaginasia' was also undertaken in Britain. With this transformation in the spectator profile of the mainstream Hindi film, one might anticipate a transformation in its cultural/political role within India as well.

Globalization and Hindi Cinema

The 1990s represent a period of transition for Hindi cinema because Nehruvian socialism ended with the economic liberalization of 1991, and Hindi cinema changed track significantly after that. Even as Hindi cinema was responding to the end of socialism, there were far-reaching developments in the social space because of the growth of new economy businesses, especially the IT/ITES sectors, and their contribution to the global economy. The new economy industries that took root in the 1990s were different in as much as their business originated abroad rather than within India. This saw Indian professionals travelling overseas as never before, and not as tourists as had once been the case. The wage levels in the new economy companies were comparable to that in the West while the cost of living remained low. This meant that employees in new economy businesses had unprecedented spending power; this resulted in an explosion in consumption and the proliferation of shopping centres and malls in the cities. Because the new businesses were global, an association was made between wealth and a working knowledge of the English language, which was the key to employment in new-economy businesses. This came to mean that the Anglophone Indian was the one with the greatest spending power. The development of India became skewed, with the new-economy businesses concentrated in the metropolitan cities. The proliferation of multiplexes in the cities (because of the new spending power) meant that the price of admission in movie houses increased in the cities but remained the same elsewhere, and Hindi cinema, therefore, began to target city audiences. With the globalization of Indian business, the Indian from the metropolises came culturally closer to those of the diaspora. Because of this factor the cultural perspective of Bollywood was also increasingly shared by South Asians outside India. Where mainstream Hindi cinema had been regarded as a pariah by the Indian State, the commercial success of Bollywood globally gave it immense respectability in the government, especially because economic factors had gained importance after 1991. Where popular Hindi cinema had once been of two identifiable kinds (mainstream and a 'B-' category as represented by the horror film) the transformation of spectator profiles has led to several identifiable kinds of Hindi cinema. These are (a) the Anglophone mainstream film as represented by *3 Idiots*, which does best in the city multiplexes; (b) the semi-urban Hindi film as represented by *Dabangg*, which uses a very local Hindi and can be termed more feudal in its attitudes and where the ruling icon after 2000 has been Salman Khan. This kind of film does well in the cities as well but this may also be on account of the large-scale migration of people to the cities. Categories (a) and (b) both continue in the Puranic narration as does category (c), which is merely a continuation of the earlier 'B' films and is represented by horror (*Raaz*, 2012) and 'hot' films which are usually unsung. The splitting up of audiences into different kinds—Anglophones from the cities, including those with global connections; the aspiring migrants from the small towns who are increasingly urban; those who remain rural or semi-urban and resistant to the global—produces a confusing array of films, which also include (d) small comedies like *Vicky Donor* (2012) and more intimate films like *Barfi!* (2012) that stand apart from both traditional art cinema and the mainstream film. The issue-based art film could itself have morphed into (d) or (e) a dramatic/realistic, but less issue-based cinema in which the most successful film-makers are those like Anurag Kashyap (*Gangs of Wasseypur*). A characteristic of this last category is its showcasing of actual locations in grimy India, suggesting its roots in the success of *Slumdog Millionaire* (2009). Some films from this category like Ritesh Batra's *The Lunchbox* (2013) also imply origins in the novel rather than mythology, since they deal with ordinary people and not heroes. This category of films has produced actors like Irrfan Khan and Nawazuddin Siddiqui, who are closer to Om Puri and Naseeruddin Shah of the 1970s art cinema than to the older stars with their theatrical gestures.

But if the above categorization suggests certainty of any kind, this is misplaced, since new stars like Ranbir Kapoor are naturalistic in their approach and play roles in all the categories. There is also such an enormous variety in the themes chosen that one cannot but speculate about what category each film belongs to. The budget of a film, however, could be a reliable indicator, and the greater difficulties pertain to identifying the categories to which the small films belong. Moreover, the increasing number of channels from which finance can be raised also makes the variety possible.

Another notable trend about the 'variety' seen in new Hindi cinema in the 'small' categories is that it is greatly indebted to the DVD revolution that has put world cinema within reach of audiences as never before. Where Hindi cinema once depended largely on Hollywood texts, films from South Korea, Iran, and France are now within reach. As just a few examples of where small Hindi films find inspiration: Navdeep Singh's *Manorama Six Feet Under* (2007) reworks Roman Polanski's *Chinatown* (1974), Sanjay Gupta's *Zinda* (2006) adapts Chan-wook Park's *Oldboy* (2003), Sagar Ballary's *Bheja Fry* (2007) is a remake of Francis Veber's *Le Dîner de Cons* (1998), and Dibakar

Banerjee's *Shanghai* (2012) draws from Costa-Gavras's *Z* (1969). One cannot always assert that the adaptations are discriminating or discerning, but what cannot be doubted is that there is enormous eclecticism on display.

While it is difficult to determine the trajectory of the Hindi film from the smaller kind of cinema, the task becomes easier when one confines oneself to the big films determined by big budgets and the presence of stars. The first aspect of this new cinema to invite attention is the weakening of melodramatic motifs, and the reason is that the moral side (implicating the notion of loyalty) is scarcely in evidence. To illustrate, friendship prevails in *3 Idiots* but loyalty to it is not brought to crisis as a melodrama might have; such films are not morally 'legible' as mainstream Hindi films inevitably were, and this can be contrasted with the friendships in *Sangam* and *Sholay*, which demand extreme sacrifices. As if to compensate, the ethic of personal aspiration has been introduced, as in *3 Idiots*, *Bunty Aur Babli*, *Guru*, and *Kaminey*. These films celebrate enterprise, but an aspect deserving special notice is that illegality is installed as a legitimate component of enterprise in *Bunty Aur Babli* and *Guru*. The mood in these films, and much more so in *Kaminey*, is celebratory when they describe 'aspirations' of this kind.

Alongside this representation of (amoral) private initiative is a denouncement of the state as corrupt. The motif of the corrupt police officer acting for his own benefit has been virtually instituted by films like *Kaminey* as filmic convention; this can be traced to the weakening of the Indian state over two decades of deregulation without a corresponding strengthening of enforcement to ensure that the laws/regulations that remained were strictly adhered to. The justification for illegality is apparently that it a global ethic since the state is shown to later enlist the fraudster protagonists of *Bunty Aur Babli* to use their expertise outside India. In *Dhoom: 2* (2006), the story begins with the protagonist stealing the British crown jewels, and the implication is that since the British 'stole' the Kohinoor diamond in the first place the act is legitimate. A contradiction often seen in these films is that they uphold illegalities but decry state corruption, and are also patriotic. It is as though unprincipled entrepreneurship can strengthen the nation, and *Guru* suggests this when the protagonist declares his intent of creating a 'world-class enterprise', and the film equates shareholder wealth in India with that of the nation. Sports films follow the same logic when sportspersons overcome obstacles created by the state and credit themselves well as in *Chak De India* (2007) and *Paan Singh Tomar* (2012). State rewards are deemed worthless, but a signing fee from a private sponsor in *Iqbal* (2005) rescues a cricketer's family from debt—acknowledgement by the market is considered more valuable than state recognition. Apart from celebrating aspiration, new cinema also takes pride in the capacity of the rich Indian to spend, especially abroad and in Europe. Many of the films appearing after 2010 make only a pretence of having a story, for instance, *ZNMD* and *Yeh Jawaani Hai Deewani* (2013) in which people splurge. The events in *Dil Dhadakne Do* (2015) occur on a Mediterranean cruise during a wedding anniversary on a rich man's yacht. Having fun is a key notion in many of these films, and this is compatible with parties, songs, dances, and foreign locations. Needless to add, these films are poor in the signifiers which might have implied the nation, since little appears to matter except romantic attachments in the midst of abundance.

This celebration of enterprise and consumption may be understood as responses to India's growth story and as may be anticipated, this cinema can be identified with broadly Anglophone audiences from the class of English speakers and users who have benefitted most from the new economy. One of the first Hindi films identifiable as with an Anglophone bias may have been *Rang De Basanti*, which also attacked politics and politicians. This anti-political stand, it can be argued, has been the cry of the upwardly mobile classes which sees politics as an impediment to economic progress, and the same view of politicians as reprehensible or self-serving continues in a host of other films that address the same kind of audiences—*Kaminey*, *Peepli Live* (2010), and *Raajneeti*. While the films are testimony to the self-absorption of the ascendant classes, in that they conduct themselves as though no other India exists, the other social segments do make occasional appearances, as in *Peepli Live*, in which indebted farmers are played by bit players and treated as subjects of anthropology rather than people with whom audiences might identify. In the earlier cinema, farmers were played heroically by stars—Nargis in *Mother India* and Manoj Kumar in *Upkaar*.

If the semi-urban Hindi blockbuster is represented most aptly by *Dabangg*, one of Salman Khan's biggest hits; which seems at first glance to be a continuation of the older Hindi cinema and feudal in its attitudes, a charge made against the traditional Hindi film by film scholars like M. Madhava Prasad. But *Dabangg* is feudal in an alarmingly new way. The protagonist of *Dabangg* is a police inspector in a small town and this sets it apart from the Anglophone Hindi film, both mainstream and small budget, in which policemen are the villains. As instances, one could cite *Kaminey*, *Drishyam* (2015), and *Masaan* (2015). In these films police officers misuse the power vested in them to further their own interests. But if in *Dabangg* the policeman is a heroic, larger-than-life figure (as would be appropriate to Puranic narration), he also misuses authority like in the other films, except that this misuse is viewed with approval. Chulbul Pandey, the protagonist of *Dabangg*, is Brahmin by birth and wears both his police uniform and caste identity with pride. It is as though both his uniform and his caste give him personal power, which he uses to his own ends, although notionally on behalf of the community. I remarked earlier that illegality becomes a legitimate component of enterprise because of the perceived weakness of the state. Here, being a representative of state authority is a legitimate path to personal power. The perception appears to be that with the state weakening, it has ceded authority or power to individuals based on their hierarchical positions in traditional society. This can be likened to collapsing empires allowing governors to assume the mantle of kings in the provinces they once administered. The alarm in this representation also comes from what it implies about the nation only 60 years after Independence.

Bollywood and the Nation

Mainstream Hindi cinema, as already demonstrated, has had an intimate relationship with the Indian nation before and since 1947. But in its avatar as Bollywood, one wonders if the relationship between the two can be as fruitful as it has been, especially since Bollywood does not represent only cinema. Many of the early debates on Hindi cinema focused on whether it was fantasy, escapism, or daydream, but as I have tried to demonstrate, it was grounded in political reality but engaged in bridging the gap between the expectations created by traditional values and beliefs and the actual dispensations of history through a kind of interpretive function. The liberal era after 1991 was, for instance, first regarded as 'Ramrajya'—society allegorized as a happy family living amidst plenty in *HAHK*—and one can see the recent celebration of upper-class lifestyles as a continuation of the same representation. But if Hindi cinema sheds its allegorical role with regard to the Indian nation, as the paucity of signifiers in recent cinema has us believe, it could eventually mean something else. A film that may especially point to Bollywood's future is a landmark release from 2007, Farah Khan's *OSO*.

OSO is set in the film industry and is about a young man Om Prakash (Shah Rukh Khan) who aspires to be a film star. This aspiration is fulfilled when he dies in a traffic accident involving Rajesh Kapoor, a major star, when he is taking his wife to a hospital for the delivery of their child; Om Prakash is reborn as his son Om Kapoor. There are other motifs in the film, including that of revenge against a movie moghul, but its most important aspect is that it showcases Bollywood as film audiences imagine it to be; film stars appear as themselves at a Filmfare Awards ceremony in which Om Kapoor is named best actor, and they behave in accordance with their public images cultivated outside cinema. As Om Prakash, Shah Rukh Khan himself does not try to act as if he is a poor, young man with aspirations, and does everything possible to don the mantle of a top entertainer, especially in a hilarious sequence in which he impersonates a south-Indian star. The entire film, it may be hazarded, resembles an ad for Shah Rukh Khan and Bollywood.

OSO perhaps represents the extreme case of the brand becoming the content but there are other indications that the meaning of popular Hindi cinema in its new avatar could well be dominated by its brand image. What this means is that considerations outside cinema dominate films and, in a sense, subvert the fiction. Here are some ways in which this process may be carried forward:

- The visibility of children or siblings of well-known stars on television long before their films actually arrive and prepare the ground for their acceptance. Stardom as inherited is hinted at in *OSO* when Om Prakash's aspirations are fulfilled only when he is reincarnated as the son of a star.
- Publicized off-screen relationships becoming an influencing factor in the writing of screenplays.

- Roles played by actors in films paralleling relationships in real life, for example, Amitabh Bachchan playing Abhishek Bachchan's father in *Kabhi Alvida Naa Kehna* (2006). When the policeman played by Amitabh lets off the criminal played by Abhishek in *Bunty Aur Babli*, it is easily read as a justification of nepotism.

- Deliberate placement of product brands within each film.

- Film costumes gradually making way for designer wear.

- Personalities cultivated in commercials informing the film, and references to them being made in the films.

- Characters in films being given the names of film stars.

- Film magazines devoted to cinema dying out, but Bollywood news (friendships, enmities, associations, relationships) and film news (releases, successes, flops, collections, and so on) becoming general news in the media, especially on television news channels.

- Elaborate fictions made about stars in advertisements that are meant to tell the public what the stars are 'really' like.

Shah Rukh Khan in *OSO* may be emblematic of what is happening to fiction in Hindi cinema, but the same is increasingly true of other performers like Aamir Khan, Akshay Kumar, and Hrithik Roshan, whose performances evoke the commercials in which they appear. Another factor to be taken into account here are the muscular bodies cultivated by the stars which are not especially justified by the fiction in the films. Where Stallone or Schwarzenegger starred in films in which their physiques are justified—the roles of boxer or robot being their best-known ones respectively—Bollywood films do not take the trouble to justify the physiques of the actors, and this means that the spectator is made aware that it is the physique of the star rather than that of a fictional character. The star persona of an actor was once also used to represent social types: the working-class hero represented by Dharmendra, the angry marginalized represented by Amitabh Bachchan, the city slicker by Dev Anand, or the impulsive and ebullient rustic by Dilip Kumar. It can be argued that if Shah Rukh Khan's star persona in *OSO* represents no social type, neither does it represent the actor as an individual. It can perhaps be described (to cite Baudrillard, 1988) as a 'simulacrum', a copy which has no corresponding original. Although popular Indian cinema was initially regarded as escapist and a 'collective daydream', these are perhaps not terms that sit comfortably on a film like *OSO*. The 'escapism' of Hindi cinema and its sententiousness both pointed to an ideal of some sort. Both owe to the understanding (shared by traditional poetics/dramaturgy) that whatever literature and performance represent should be 'truer than the real'. Or, seen from an external perspective, it was a tidied-up copy of what is real in the world. It is because the world of *OSO* is part of a collapsed fiction that it is not a tidied up copy but closer to 'hyperreal', to use Baudrillard's words. It is difficult to say in what direction Bollywood will take Indian cinema, but an aspect of the greatest importance is that it could actually disengage Hindi cinema from the nation. It can be proposed that while the Hindi popular film once exercised influence on behalf of India (partly in the Third World), Bollywood could eventually become an advertisement for itself; reconfiguring itself as a lifestyle platform—and not as national cinema—might be the first step.

Bibliography

Anderson, Arthur. 2001. *Indian Entertainment Industry: Envisioning for Tomorrow.* New Delhi: Federation of Indian Chambers of Commerce and Industry.

Anderson, Benedict. 1983. *Imagined Communities: Reflections on the Origin and Spread of Nationalism.* London: Verso Books.

Armes, Roy. 1974. *Film and Reality: A Historical Survey.* Harmondsworth: Penguin Books.

Barthes, Roland. 1973. 'Myth Today', in *Mythologies.* London: Paladin Press, pp. 109–59.

————. 1977. *Image, Music, Text*, tr. Stephen Heath. London: Fontana Books.

Baudrillard, Jean. 1988. 'Simulacra and Simulations', in *Jean Baudrillard: Selected Writings.* Stanford: Stanford University Press, pp. 166–84.

Baumer, Rachel M. Van and Brandon R. James (eds). 1993. *Sanskrit Drama in Performance.* Delhi: Motilal Banarsidass.

Berkson, Carmel. 2000. *The Life of Form in Indian Sculpture.* Delhi: Abhiman Publications.

Bordwell, David. 1985. *Narration in the Fiction Film.* London: Methuen Publishing.

————. 2000. *Planet Hong Kong: Popular Cinema and the Art of Entertainment.* Cambridge: Harvard University Press.

Bordwell, David, Janet Staiger, and Kristin Thompson. 1985. *The Classical Hollywood Cinema: Film Style and Mode of Production to 1960.* London: Routledge & Kegan Paul.

Braudy, Leo. 1976. *The World in a Frame: What We See in Films.* New York: Doubleday.

Brooks, Peter. 1985. *The Melodramatic Imagination: Balzac, Henry James, Melodrama, and the Mode of Excess.* New York: Columbia University Press.

Byrski, M. Christopher. 1993. 'Sanskrit Drama as an Aggregate of Model Situations', in Rachel Van M. Baumer and James R. Brandon (eds), *Sanskrit Drama in Performance.* New Delhi: Motilal Banarsidass, pp. 114–66.

Chabria, Suresh (ed.). 1994. *Light of Asia: Indian Silent Cinema, 1912–1934.* Pune: National Film Archive of India.

Chakravarty, Sumita S. 1996. *National Identity in Indian Popular Cinema, 1947–1987.* New Delhi: Oxford University Press.

Chaudhuri, Nirad C. 1979. *Hinduism.* New York: Oxford University Press.

Das, Durga. 1973. *India: From Curzon to Nehru and After.* New Delhi: Rupa Publications.

Das, Veena. 1980. 'The Mythological Film and Its Framework of Meaning: An Analysis of *Jai Santoshi Maa*', in *India International Centre Quarterly* (Special Issue), 8 (1): 43–56.

Dasgupta, S.N. 1954. *Fundamentals of Indian Art*. New Delhi: Bharatiya Vidya Bhavan.

Das Gupta, Chidananda. 1991. *The Painted Face: Studies in India's Popular Cinema*. New Delhi: Roli Books.

Desai, Meghnad. 1975. 'India: Contradictions of Slow Capitalist Development', in Robin Blackburn (ed.), *Explosion in a Subcontinent*. London: Penguin Books, pp. 11–51.

Deutsch, Eliot. 1993. 'Reflections on Some Aspects of the Theory of Rasa', in Rachel M. Van Baumer and James R. Brandon (eds), *Sanskrit Drama in Performance*. Delhi: Motilal Banarsidass, pp. 207–38.

Ganti, Tejaswini. 2004. *Bollywood: A Guidebook to Popular Hindi Cinema*. New York: Routledge.

Gargi, Balwant. 1991a. *Folk Theatre of India*. Kolkata: Rupa Publications.

———. 1991b. *Folk Theatre of India*. Kolkata: Rupa Publications.

Gerow, Edwin. 1977. *Indian Poetics*. Wiesbaden: Otto Harrassowitz.

Gopalan, Lalitha. 2000. 'Avenging Women in Indian Cinema', in Ravi Vasudevan (ed.), *Making Meaning in Indian Cinema*. New Delhi: Oxford University Press, pp. 215–37.

—————. 2002. *Cinema of Interruptions: Action Genres in Contemporary Indian Cinema*. London: British Film Institute.

Hu, Brian. 2006. *Bollywood Dreaming:* Kal Ho Naa Ho *and the Diasporic Spectator*. FPO: IP Research and Communities.

Jameson, Frederic. 1987. 'Third World Literature in the Age of Multi-National Capitalism', in Clayton Kolb and Virgil Lokke (eds), *The Current in Criticism: Essays on the Present and Future of Literary Theory*. West Lafayette: Purdue University Press, pp. 131–63.

—————. 1988. 'Postmodernism and Consumer Society', in E. Ann Kaplan (ed.), *Postmodernism and Its Discontents*. London: Verso Books, pp. 13–29.

—————. 1991. *Postmodernism: Or, the Cultural Logic of Late Capitalism*. Durham: Duke University Press.

Kabir, Nasreen Munni. 1999. *Talking Films: Conversations on Hindi Cinema with Javed Akhtar*. New Delhi: Oxford University Press.

Kakar, Sudhir. 1989. *Intimate Relations: Exploring Indian Sexuality*. New Delhi: Penguin Books.

Kapur, Anuradha. 1993. 'The Representation of Gods and Heroes: Parsi Mythological Drama of the Early Twentieth Century', *Journal of Arts and Ideas*, 23–4 (January): 85–107.

Kaviraj, Sudipta. 1986. 'Indira Gandhi and Indian Politics', *Economic and Political Weekly*, 21 (38–9): 1697–708.

Khilnani, Sunil. 1998. *The Idea of India*. New Delhi: Penguin Books.

Landy, Marcia (ed.). 1991. *Imitations of Life: A Reader on Film, Television and Melodrama*. Detroit: Wayne University Press.

Lannoy, Richard. 1971. *The Speaking Tree: A Study of Indian Culture and Society*. New York: Oxford University Press.

Livingston, Paisley. 1996. 'Characterization and Fictional Truth', in David Bordwell and Noel Carroll (eds), *Post Theory: Reconstructing Film Studies*. Madison: The University of Wisconsin Press, pp. 149–74.

Lutgendorf, Philip. 2002. '"A Made for Satisfaction Goddess": Jai Santoshi Maa Revisited', part 2, *Manushi*, 131: 24–37.

Lyman, Stanford M. 1992. 'The Road to Anhedonia: Patterns of Emotional Conflict in American Films, 1930–1988', in *Social Perspectives on Emotion: A Research Annual*, vol. I. Greenwich: Jai Press Inc., pp. 170–95.

Macdonell, Arthur A. 1958. *A History of Sanskrit Literature*. New Delhi: Munshiram Manoharlal.

Majumdar, Neepa. 2001. 'The Embodied Voice: Song Sequences and Stardom in Popular Hindi Cinema', in Pamela Robertson Wojcik and Arthur Knight (eds), *Soundtrack Available: Essays on Film and Popular Music*. Durham: Duke University Press, pp. 161–83.

Majumdar, R.C., H.C. Vasudevan, and Ravi Vasudevan. 2000. 'Shifting Codes, Dissolving Identities: The Hindi

Popular Film of the 1950s as Popular Culture', in Ravi Vasudevan (ed.), *Making Meaning in Indian Cinema*. Delhi: Oxford University Press, pp. 99–121.

Mishra, Vijay. 1985. 'Towards a Theoretical Critique of Bombay Cinema', *Screen*, 26 (3–4): 133–46.

————. 2002. *Bollywood Cinema: Temples of Desire*. London: Routledge.

Monaco, James. 1981. *How to Read a Film: The Art, Technology, Language, History, and Theory of Film and Media*. New York: Oxford University Press.

Nandy, Ashis. 1980a. 'The Popular Hindi Film: Ideology and First Principles', *India International Center Quarterly* (Special Issue), 8 (1): 89–96.

————. 1980b. *At the Edge of Psychology*. New Delhi: Oxford University Press.

————. 1983. *The Intimate Enemy: Loss and Recovery of Self under Colonialism*. New Delhi: Oxford University Press.

————. 1987. 'An Intelligent Critic's Guide to Indian Cinema', *Deep Focus*, 1 (1): 68–72.

Oommen, M.A. and K.V. Joseph. 1991. *Economics of Indian Cinema*. New Delhi: Oxford University Press and IBH Publishing Co. Pvt. Ltd.

Pfleiderer, Beatrix. 1985. 'An Empirical Study of Urban and Semi-Urban Audience Reaction to Hindi Films', in Beatrix Pfleiderer and Lothar Lutze (eds), *The Hindi Film: Agent and Re-Agent of Cultural Change*. Delhi: Manohar Publications, pp. 81–130.

Pfleiderer, Beatrix and Lothar Lutze (eds). 1985. *The Hindi Film: Agent and Re-Agent of Cultural Change*. Delhi: Manohar Publications.

Pinney, Christopher. 1997. *Camera Indica: The Social Life of Indian Photographs*. Chicago: University of Chicago Press.

Prasad, M. Madhava. 1998. *Ideology of the Hindi Film: A Historical Construction*. New Delhi: Oxford University Press.

Punathambekar, Ashwin. 2013. *From Bombay to Bollywood: The Making of a Global Media Industry*. New York: New York University Press.

Raghavendra, M.K. 1992. 'Time and the Popular Film', *Deep Focus*, 4 (1): 10–18.

———. 2008. *Seduced by the Familiar: Narration and Meaning in Indian Popular Cinema*. New Delhi: Oxford University Press.

———. 2009. 'Social Dystopia or Entrepreneurial Fantasy: The Significance of Kaminey', *Economic and Political Weekly*, 44 (38): 15–17.

———. 2010a. 'India, Higher Education and Bollywood', *Economic and Political Weekly*, 45 (10): 30–2.

———. 2010b. 'Peepli Live and the Gesture of Concern', *Economic and Political Weekly*, 45 (39): 13–15.

———. 2011a. 'Zindagi Na Milegi Dobara, Delhi Belly and the Imagined Nation', *Economic and Political Weekly*, 46 (36): 27–9.

————. 2011b. *Bipolar Identity: Region, Nation and the Kannada Language Film*. New Delhi: Oxford University Press.

————. 2011c. *The Politics of Hindi Cinema in the New Millennium: Bollywood and the Anglophone Indian Nation*. New Delhi: Oxford University Press.

————. 2012. 'Paan Singh Tomar, the Nation and the Sportsperson', *Economic and Political Weekly*, 47 (17): 20–2.

Rajadhyaksha, Ashish. 1987. 'The Phalke Era: Conflict of Traditional Form and Modern Technology', *Journal of Arts and Ideas*, vol. no. 14–15: 79–107.

————. 2000. 'Viewership and Democracy in the Cinema', in Ravi Vasudevan (ed.), *Making Meaning in Indian Cinema*. New Delhi: Oxford University Press, pp. 267–96.

————. 2009. *Indian Cinema in the Time of Celluloid: From Bollywood to the Emergency*. New Delhi: Tulika Books.

Rajadhyaksha, Ashish and Paul Willemen. 1985. *Encyclopaedia of Indian Cinema*. New Delhi: Oxford University Press.

Majumdar, R.C., H.C. Raychaudhuri, and Kalikinkar Datta 1983. *An Advanced History of India*. Delhi: Macmillan.

Rowland, Benjamin. 1967. *The Art and Architecture of India*. Baltimore: Penguin Books.

Schatz, Thomas. 1999. 'Film Genre and the Genre Film', in Leo Braudy and Marshall Cohen (eds), *Film Theory and Criticism: Introductory Readings*. New York: Oxford University Press, pp. 642–53.

Shekar, Indu. 1977. *Sanskrit Drama, Its Origin and Decline*. Delhi: Munshiram Manoharlal.

Spear, Percival. 1970. *A History of India*, vol. 2. Harmondsworth: Penguin Books.

Thomas, Rosie. 1985. 'Indian Cinema: Pleasures and Popularity', *Screen* 26 (3–4): 116–31.

Index

About the Author

M.K. Raghavendra is a film scholar and a founder editor of *Phalanx*, a web journal dedicated to debate. He received the Swarna Kamal for the Best Film Critic at the 1997 National Film Awards. He was awarded a two-year Homi Bhabha Fellowship in 2000–1 to research Indian popular film narrative, as well as a Goethe-Insitut Fellowship in 2000 to study post-war German cinema. He has authored books on academic film criticism, such as *Directors Cut: 50 Major Filmmakers of the Modern Era* (2013), *Bipolar Identity: Region, Nation, and the Kannada Language Film* (2011), *50 Indian Film Classics* (2009), and *Seduced by the Familiar: Narration and Meaning in Indian Popular Cinema* (2008). *Seduced by the Familiar and 50 Indian Film Classics* have been recognized as among the best books on cinema from around the world by Fédération Internationale de la Presse Cinématographique, the International Federation of Film Critics. His academic essays on Indian cinema have been published in Indian and international anthologies.